The Complete
POULTRY
Cookbook

by Lonnie Gandara
with Peggy Fallon

HPBooks
a division of
PRICE STERN SLOAN
Los Angeles

Photography and food styling by Burke/Triolo Photographic Studio.

Some accessories for photography were from Buddy's, Los Angeles; Prince's Table, Los Angeles; Cottura, Los Angeles; Wilder Place, Los Angeles and The Pavilion at Tanner Market, Pasadena, California.

Cover photo is Grilled Game Hens with Rhubarb & Raspberry Coulis, page 105.

Published by HPBooks, a division of Price Stern Sloan, Inc.
360 North La Cienega Boulevard, Los Angeles, California 90048

© 1990 Lonnie Gandara
Printed in U.S.A.

10 9 8 7 6 5 4 3 2 1

Gandara, Lonnie.
    The complete poultry cookbook / by Lonnie Gandara
and Peggy Fallon.
       p. cm.
    ISBN 0-89586-694-3
    1. Cookery (Poultry)   I. Title.
TX750.G36   1990
641.6'65—dc20   89-19797
                          CIP

CONTENTS

Lonnie Gandara is an author, lecturer, food consultant and vice-president of a national corporation. She lives and works in San Francisco.

Originally from St. Joseph, Missouri, she has travelled extensively throughout the world and studied cooking in such places as Bangkok, Hong Kong, Italy, Istanbul, Mexico and Singapore. While living in France she earned an Advanced Certificate from Le Cordon Bleu and was graduated from L'Academie du Vin.

Over the past 13 years Lonnie has organized and chaired numerous food-related events, including the Culinary Carnival Great Party, the San Francisco March of Dimes Gourmet Gala, the Gourmet Products Show, the International Wine and Food Show and the Source Fair for the Fourth Annual Symposium on American Cuisine. As food consultant for Macys California, she produced such events as the Great Chefs of San Francisco, the James Beard Birthday Party with American Express, Famous Chef Seminars and Cookware Weeks.

She has authored three other cookbooks: *Fish and Shellfish, Ice Cream and Other Frozen Desserts and 365 Great Barbecue and Grilling Recipes.*

A native Californian and long-time associate of Ms. Gandara, **Peggy Fallon** is a former caterer who now develops recipes, writes and teaches cooking in the San Francisco Bay Area. She is known for her menus for entertaining, which stress advance preparation and creative presentation. Having been born on Thanksgiving Day, she holds a lifelong fondness for turkey.

Both Lonnie and Peggy are members of the International Association of Cooking Professionals, the American Institute of Wine and Food and the San Francisco Professional Food Society.

INTRODUCTION

*W*hether you shop at the neighborhood butcher or a big city market, the array of poultry can be staggering.

In addition to the predictable whole chickens, we can find halves and quarters, breasts, thighs, drumsticks, wings, backs, necks, gizzards, livers and hearts. Turkeys are further divided in steaks, cutlets, tenderloins and fillets. Even ground turkey and chicken are available. Turkey sausage substitutes for pork, and turkey can also be found in nearly all varieties of cured and processed meats on the market today.

Duck has been appreciated for centuries by the French and Chinese, and now it's finally coming into its own in the United States. Unfortunately too many "continental" restaurants have done a disservice to this bird by burying a fatty piece of meat beneath a too-sweet sauce.

Duck is indeed fatty, but more than half the calories are in the skin. It is more expensive than other fowl due to the low proportion of edible meat to fat and bone, but the unique treat of juicy red meat combined with the crisp skin is making duck a popular choice for today. Duck parts are becoming more available throughout the country.

Geese may need to be special ordered at times other than the holidays. These dark-fleshed birds are also fatty, but provide an interesting change from the usual and a memorable taste treat.

Just as wild mushrooms are no longer necessarily "wild," game birds are not necessarily hunted. Game farms make these birds available all year round. Small game birds cook quickly, making them convenient to prepare. Though once thought of as cold-weather fare, the meat of these farmed birds is extremely lean, making it ideal for warm weather dining. Add game birds to your diet for a flavorful change of pace.

Poultry is the low-fat, low-calorie, versatile choice for today's cook.

Cobb Salad, page 41

Type	Description	Age
CHICKEN		
Poussin	full breasted immature chicken	under 6 weeks
Rock Cornish game hen	immature chicken/special breed	4-5 weeks
Broiler	young chicken of either sex	7-9 weeks
Fryer	young chicken of either sex	9-12 weeks
Roaster	young chicken of either sex	10-20 weeks
Capon	young chicken, surgically neutered male, meat is tender but less flavorful	16-20 weeks
Stewing chicken	mature female chicken	over 10 months

Clockwise from top left: Capon, Roaster, Stewing chicken, Fryer, Broiler and Rock Cornish Game hens

POULTRY PRIMER

Type	Description	Age
TURKEY		
Fryer-roaster	young immature turkey	under 16 weeks
Young turkey		
Hen	female young turkey	14-22 weeks
Tom	male young turkey (larger than female; otherwise the same)	14-22 weeks
Mature turkey	fully matured turkey, more meat to the bone, but less flavorful	over 15 months
OTHER		
Duckling/duck		7-16 weeks
Goose		over 6 months
Pheasant		6 weeks
Squab		under 6 weeks
Quail		under 6 weeks

Clockwise from top left: Turkey, Goose, Duck, Pheasant, Squabs and Quail

BUYING INFORMATION

Type	Weight	How much to buy
CHICKEN		
Poussin	1 lb.	½ to 1 bird per person
Rock Cornish game hen	under 2 lbs.	½ to 1 bird per person
Broiler	1½-2½ lbs.	½ lb. per serving
Fryer	3-4 lbs.	½ lb. per serving
Roaster	4-7 lbs.	½ lb. per serving
Capon	6-9 lbs.	½ lb. per serving
Stewing chicken	3-7 lbs.	½ lb. per serving
TURKEY		
Fryer-roaster	4-8 lbs.	¾ lb. per serving
Young turkey		
Hen	7-15 lbs.	½ to 1 lb. per serving
Tom	15-25 lbs.	½ to 1 lb. per serving
Mature turkey	12-25 lbs.	½ to 1 lb. per serving
OTHER		
Duckling/duck	3-5½ lbs.	½ duck per person
Goose	4-14 lbs.	1 to 1½ lbs. per person
Pheasant	2-3 lbs.	1 to 1½ lbs. per person
Squab	¾-1 lb.	1 to 2 birds per person
Quail	¼-½ lb.	2 to 3 birds per person

POULTRY POINTERS

When selecting poultry, look for a plump full-breasted bird with smooth, unblemished skin, clean smell and a minimum of pinfeathers. As a bird matures, the top of its cartilaginous keel (breastbone) calcifies and becomes brittle. Look for flexible breastbones in chickens and turkey and pliable bills in ducks and geese.

Years ago, yellow skin guaranteed extra flavor and surface fat due to the bird's nutritious diet and its exposure to sunlight and plants. Within the last 20 years, with the increased demand for poultry, the bluish-white skin of mass produced birds is hidden by feeding them formula rich in marigold petals or other sources of carotene.

Sometimes the flesh and leg bone of a fully cooked young or previously frozen chicken will appear reddish because the hemoglobin (red pigment in blood) contained within the bones leaches out after cooking. This hemoglobin is edible and harmless, so there is no need to return the chicken to the oven for unnecessary cooking.

Poultry is a high-quality source of protein, and is low in sodium, saturated fats and cholesterol, with turkey being the leanest of all. Fat and cholesterol are reduced even more if the skin and visible fat are removed before cooking.

To freeze chicken, remove and discard the store's wrapping material and wrap airtight in heavy-duty foil or freezer paper. Poultry may be frozen up to nine months.

THAWING TIPS

• Thaw frozen poultry in its original wrapper, placed in a clean tray or pan in the refrigerator overnight. As a general rule, you can plan for about 24 hours thawing time for every five pounds of poultry weight. For large turkeys, allow several days in the refrigerator for thorough and safe defrosting.

• To thaw in a microwave oven, follow the manufacturer's instructions.

• When thawing poultry in the refrigerator, place in a pan or bowl to prevent liquid from the thawing poultry dripping on other food in the refrigerator and contaminating it.

• Never thaw poultry at room temperature. To thaw poultry quickly, place it in its original wrapping and/or a water-tight bag and place it in COLD water, changing the water about every 30 minutes. Large turkeys will take 6 to 12 hours to thoroughly defrost.

IS CHICKEN REALLY A DANGEROUS BIRD?

The chickens we eat now are produced and processed under far more sanitary conditions than ever before. However there is public concern about food poisoning caused by salmonella found in chicken. Salmonella is a common and natural microorganism present everywhere in our environment, and not just in poultry. Chicken is less frequently a source of salmonellosis (the flu-like illness caused by salmonella) than other meats because it is never eaten raw and seldom undercooked.

Food Safety Tips

• Thoroughly cook meat until it is no longer pink and the juices run clear when pierced with a fork.

• Rinse all poultry, whole or cut up, with cold water and pat dry prior to cooking.

• Cooked chicken should be stored in the coldest part of your refrigerator (below 40F) and should be kept no longer than two to three days after purchase.

• Thaw poultry properly. (See Thawing Tips, opposite.)

• Never stuff a bird and then freeze it.

• Always wash your work surface, utensils and hands with soap and hot water before and after working with uncooked chicken.

CUTTING UP CHICKENS

Judging from the price differential between whole and cut up chickens in the supermarket, it seems butchers want us to believe that there is some incredible mystique involved in cutting up a bird. Nonsense. Anyone with a sharp knife can disjoint a chicken into serving pieces in less than five minutes.

When whole chickens are on special at the market, buy as many as you'll be able to use over the next few weeks. Disjointing several birds at one time goes remarkably fast when you create an assembly-line system. Package the parts according to your personal preferences.

The following waste-free method of cutting up a bird is not only economical, it provides serving pieces that appear far more appetizing than those massacred with a buzz saw! You will probably disjoint chickens most often, but the basic principles apply to all poultry.

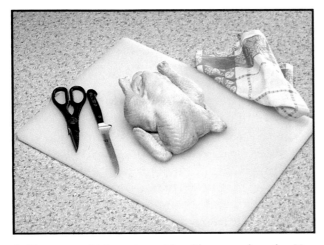

1. To cut up a chicken, rinse with cold water and pat dry. Use either kitchen shears or a knife or both. Do not use a wooden cutting board.

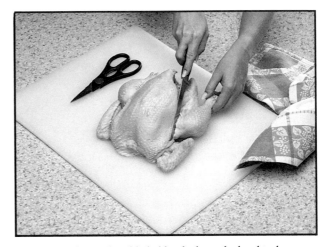

2. Insert a sharp, thin-bladed knife through the skin between the leg and body, down through the thigh joint.

3. After dislocating the joint with your hands, insert knife between the ball and socket of the joint and separate by pulling and cutting. Separate drumstick and thigh. Repeat with other leg.

4. Pull wing away from body and use a sharp knife to cut down through to free the joint, cutting away a bit of the breast meat at the same time. Repeat with other wing.

In Ten Easy Pieces

Remove neck and giblets from cavity and reserve for other uses. Rinse chicken with cold water and pat dry.

Insert a sharp, thin-bladed knife through the skin between the leg and body, down through to the thigh joint. Grasp the drumstick with your other hand, using a paper towel if slippery, and dislocate the joint by bending the entire leg backwards until the ball of the thighbone pops from the hip socket. Insert knife between the ball and socket of the joint. Separate the thigh portion of the leg from the bird by pulling and cutting, if necessary. Repeat with other leg.

Lay the legs skin-side down on cutting board. Locate the thin line of fat that runs crosswise along the flesh between the drumstick and thigh. Cut down along the line of fat on a 45 degree angle to separate the drumstick and thigh.

Pull wing away from body and use a sharp knife to cut down through and free the joint, cutting away a bit of the breast meat at the same time. Repeat with other wing.

Separate the whole breast from the backbone by cutting along both sides of the ribcage with a knife or kitchen shears. Detach by pulling the breast and back apart from each other and cutting through the shoulder blades. Divide back horizontally by cutting across where the ribcage ends. Place breast skin-side down. Cut lengthwise through the white cartilage to the neck-end of the breastbone. Bend breast back, exposing the coarse end of bone by running thumb or index finger around it. Pull out bone. (If cartilage snaps off, it can easily be removed with a knife.) Use knife to vertically divide breast into equal halves. The breasts of large birds can be cut again crosswise to yield four to six breast portions.

5. Separate the whole breast from the backbone by cutting along both sides of the ribcage with a knife or kitchen shears. Detach by pulling the breast and back apart from each other and cutting through the shoulder blades.

6. Divide back horizontally by cutting across where the ribcage ends.

7. Place breast skin-side down. Bend breast back, exposing the coarse end of bone by running thumb or index finger around it. Pull out bone. If cartilage snaps off, remove with a knife. Cut breast vertically into equal halves.

8. A whole chicken yields 10 pieces. Here half the breast is also shown with the bone removed.

In Halves or Quarters

Place the bird breast-side down on a cutting board. Starting at the neck end, use a sharp knife to cut down through one side of the backbone to the tail.

Pull the chicken open and remove the backbone by cutting down the other side of the backbone from the neck to tail with a knife or kitchen shears. Reserve backbone for soup. Remove the breastbone by bending breast back and running your thumb under the bone. Lift out to remove, as shown for cutting up a chicken (see page 13). Cut through the center of breast to halve the bird.

To cut halves into quarters, position the knife at the base of the rib section on a slight angle. Cut through the piece just below the ribs to divide the wing/breast section from the drumstick/thigh.

1. Place the chicken breast-side down on a cutting board. Starting at the neck end, use a sharp knife to cut down through one side of the backbone to the tail.

2. Pull chicken open and remove the backbone by cutting down its other side with kitchen shears. Remove breast bone as on page 13.

3. Cut vertically through the center of the breast to halve the chicken.

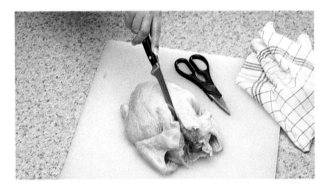

4. To cut into quarters, continue by positioning your knife at the base of the rib section on a slight angle. Cut just below the ribs to divide the wing and breast from the drumstick and thigh.

Boning a Chicken Breast

A whole breast is boned in the same manner as the breast on a whole bird (page 13). To bone a half-breast, insert the point of a knife along the wider edge of the breast (pointing toward the center), between the flesh and bone.

With the blade of the knife resting flat against the bone, use a gentle up and down sawing motion to release the meat, moving the knife gradually from one end of the breast to the other. Use your hands to pull the breast meat away from the bone, using the point of your knife to free the meat from the rib cage, if necessary. Reserve bones for stock.

How To Cook Poultry

All cooking methods fall within one of two categories: moist and dry. The U.S. Department of Agriculture has established guidelines and classifications for poultry. These classifications are associated with physical characteristics as well as age (see Poultry Primer, pages 8 and 9), and therefore provide clues as to the best cooking methods to use.

Moist cooking can be used with any poultry, but is ideally suited to older birds whose tough flesh is high on flavor, though low in tenderness. Steamed poultry is cooked above the cooking liquid, while stews, braised dishes and poached fowl are cooked directly in it. This same cooking liquid becomes part of the completed dish when it is used for braising or stewing, but not when poaching and steaming.

Frying

When the liquid into which poultry is submerged is oil, the process is called deep-frying. The success of this fast and efficient technique is dependent upon the proper temperature of the oil, anywhere from 350F (175C) to 400F (205C). A lower temperature takes longer to cook and usually guarantees that the food will absorb more oil and become soggy. Oil that is too hot will burn and convey a scorched taste to the food.

Vegetable oils seem to work best for deep-frying. Oil can be used one or two times, if desired, but it does retain flavors and eventually breaks down. To save oil for reuse, pour it through a sieve lined with cheesecloth or a paper towel, or a paper coffee filter. Cover and store in the refrigerator until ready to use. When deep-frying, make sure the pan you are using is heavy and well balanced. Woks work particularly well, because their sloped sides mean you require less oil. Don't crowd the food to be fried. Cook in several batches if necessary, allowing the oil to return to the original temperature before beginning the next batch. Handle food with a clean, dry slotted spoon, long handled tongs, or the wire strainers available in Asian markets. Deep fried food should be drained on paper towels before being served.

A good-quality deep-fat thermometer is a wise investment for anyone who even occasionally employs this type of cookery. If you deep-fry foods frequently, invest in a thermostatically controlled electric deep-fat fryer.

Lacking such conveniences, a test for determining the temperature of oil is to time how long it takes a 1-inch cube of bread to turn golden-brown after being dropped into the hot oil.

Sautéing and stir-frying each use a very small amount of fat that often becomes part of the

Deep-Fat Frying Temperatures

If the bread cube turns golden in:	*The temperature of the oil is:*
65 seconds	345F to 355F (175C)
60 seconds	356F to 365F (180C)
50 seconds	366F to 375F (185C)
40 seconds	376F to 385F (190C)
20 seconds	386F to 395F (200C)

finished dish. Using high temperatures for a short cooking time seals in the flavor and moisture of young succulent birds. Broiling and grilling are other high heat methods best suited to young birds in even, manageable pieces.

SMOKE COOKING

Smoke cooking refers to smoking at a temperature high enough to cook the food that is being smoked. If you are interested in smoking your own poultry, buy or build a smoker and follow the instructions appropriate to your model. This type of cooking costs a fraction of what you would pay for commercially smoked poultry, and is ideal for those who love the smoky flavor of outdoor cooking but hate standing over a hot grill.

ROASTING & BAKING

Roasting and baking are probably the most common methods of cooking with dry heat. The term roasting generally refers to the cooking method used for a whole bird. When cooking casseroles or pieces of poultry that have already been cut into serving-size portions, the process is described as baking.

There are different schools of thought on the pros and cons of roasting at high (400F/205C) or medium (325F/265C) heat. Roasting at a high temperature concentrates flavor in the juicy interior, while the exterior browns nicely. Shrinkage is relatively high with this method, and the bird usually renders only a few tablespoons of drippings for gravy. Roasting at the lower temperature allows juices to escape since the exterior won't be sealed as quickly, making for a slightly drier bird. This also means there will be plenty of drippings for a flavorful gravy, however, and the bird will remain plump because shrinkage will be at a minimum.

Spit-roasting indoors or out is an ideal method, as the constant rotation releases any steam rising from the joints into the air. In an oven, this steam condenses and creates moisture which is counter productive to roasting and sealing in the juices. Allow approximately 25 minutes per pound for an unstuffed bird.

When roasting in an oven, large turkeys cook better at 325F (165C) as this ensures the progressive penetration of heat to the center. A hot oven browns the exterior of the bird before the center is fully cooked.

Roasting Tips
• Place a bird on a rack inside the roasting pan so it won't pan-fry in its own fat and overcook.

• Baste with melted butter, oil or rendered chicken fat (page 22). Other liquids produce steam and delay the caramelization process. You may want to try any of the compound butters (see pages 136 to 137) or the Garlic Oil (see page 21).

• Ducks and geese are considered red meat and therefore do well when roasted at higher temperatures.

• Because they are basically fatty, ducks and geese do not need to be basted with additional oil or fat. Prior to roasting, pierce duck or goose skin (not the flesh) all over with a fork. Also, it's not a good idea to stuff these birds with bread or rice, as they tend to absorb the fat from the inside.

• Instead of stuffing birds, fill the cavities with aromatic herbs, onions or citrus slices. This will impart a heavenly aroma and subtle flavor, and will cook faster than a stuffed bird.

• When filling a bird with a stuffing to be eaten, fill the cavity *just* before cooking. Stuffing the bird for as little as 15 minutes in advance may create a health hazard. Once a stuffed bird has been roasted, remove *all* of the stuffing immediately.

Poultry Roasting Timetable

Minutes per Pound   Internal Temperature Readings

ROASTING AT 400F (205C) (High Temperature Method)

Chicken and game birds.......18* ....170F (75C) Breast, 185F (85C) Thigh
Duck...............................15* ....180F (80C) Thigh
Goose..............................18* ....185F (85C) Thigh

ROASTING AT 325F (165C) (Medium Temperature Method)

Chicken and game birds.......25* ....170F (75C) Breast, 185F (85C) Thigh
Duck...............................25* ....180F (80C) Thigh
Goose..............................25* ....185F (85C) Thigh
Turkey.............................15 to 20..........................170F (75C) Breast, 185F (85C) Thigh

*Note: If poultry is stuffed, add 20 to 30 minutes to the total cooking time.
Stuffing should reach a temperature of 165F (75C).

1. Spoon stuffing lightly into poultry cavities just prior to roasting. Do not pack stuffing tightly.

2. Use your fingers to loosen skin from body. Spread butter, herbs or stuffing under skin to add flavor.

1. Cut strips of parchment paper, 11 inches long and 1-1/2 inches wide. Fold in half lengthwise. Make cuts along fold about 1/4 inch apart and half the width of the paper. Refold paper so original fold is inside and tape along edge.

2. Attach ruffles to roasted turkey legs by wrapping around joint as shown. Secure ends with tape.

To Truss. . . Or Not

The main advantage to trussing poultry is that it makes for a more appetizing presentation. Also, when the legs are bound tightly to the body, the cavity is better suited for holding stuffing.

Testing has shown that birds cook evenly with or without trussing, so the option is yours. Some cooks prefer to secure the bird's cavities with the small metal skewers available in the housewares section of most grocery stores. Others truss using a long needle with an eye large enough to hold the string, but the same effect can be had by using a yard-long piece of cotton kitchen twine.

Remove neck, liver, giblets and excess fat from the cavity and reserve for other uses.

Removing the wishbone from the neck cavity expands the area for stuffing and simplifies carving later. To remove the wishbone, fold back the neck skin and cut all around the bone with a small, sharp knife. Using your fingers, pull the bone toward you to free it from the flesh. Stuff neck cavity, if desired, and pull the flap of excess skin over the opening and close securely by tucking the wings under the breast. If breast cavity is to be stuffed, do it at this time.

Trussing with String

Position a yard-long piece of kitchen string under the center of the neck-end of the bird and pull the twine forward and under the drumsticks and tail. Crisscross the string to hold the tail in an upright position.

Loop the ends of string around the ends of the drumsticks to pull them in close to the body. Draw the string tightly and tie a single knot to pull the drumsticks close together. Take the ends of the string and bring back toward neck-end by running them in close between the breast and drumsticks. Pull the ends of string together at the neck-end where you began and tie securely beneath the bird.

To Carve A Turkey— Or Other Fowl

Few hosts are able to carry off the logistical nightmare of engaging in spirited conversation with family and friends while effortlessly carving a whole bird perched on a slippery china platter.

The most practical and relaxed means of carving is accomplished on a cutting board in the kitchen, with the finished product presented to guests on a clean serving platter, attractively garnished with crisp sprigs of fresh parsley or watercress.

Chicken and capons are handled essentially the same as turkey, while game hens are generally cut in half or served whole, like quail. The procedures for carving chicken, capons, ducks and

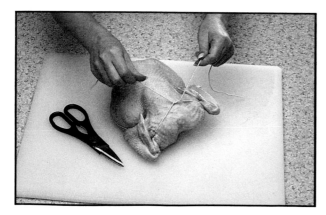

1. Position a yard-long piece of kitchen string under the center of the neck-end of the bird and pull the string forward and under the drumsticks and tail. Crisscross the string to hold the tail in an upright position. Loop the ends of string around the ends of the drumsticks and pull them in close to the body. Tie a single knot to pull the drumsticks close together.

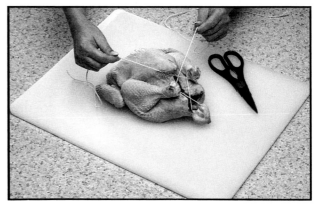

2. Take the ends of the string and bring back toward neck-end by running them in close between the breast and drumsticks. Pull the ends of string together at the neck-end where you began and tie securely beneath the bird.

1. It's much easier to carve a roasted turkey in the kitchen than in the dining room. Use a two-tined fork and a 9- to 14-inch slicing knife. Using the fork to steady the bird, cut the skin between the right leg and the body to locate the leg joint. Cut through joint to remove leg and thigh. Repeat with other leg.

2. Slice through the edge of the breast down through the shoulder joint. Remove the wing with the small amount of breast attached.

geese follow the basic procedures for turkey outlined below.

In any case, poultry should rest prior to carving so juices can recirculate and settle. Allow at least 15 minutes for small birds and 30 minutes for large ones.

Begin with a two-tined fork and a 9- to 14-inch slicing knife with a flexible blade and a very sharp edge. Cut away the trussing string, if any, and discard. If there is stuffing, remove all of it to a warm serving bowl. Lay the turkey breast-side up on a carving board. Using the fork to steady the bird, cut the skin between the right leg and the body to locate the leg joint. Cut through the joint—all the way through the bird, to disconnect the leg and thigh. Repeat on the left side.

Place the leg/thigh portions on the cutting board, skin-side up. Slice through the joint to separate the drumstick from the thigh, and then slice the meat from both pieces and place on a serving platter. Reserve bones for soup or stock.

Slice through the edge of the breast down through the shoulder joint.

Remove the wing with the small piece of breast meat attached and place on a serving platter. Repeat on other side.

Remove each half breast by inserting the point of your knife along the upper ridge of the breastbone, following its contour while keeping the flat side of the knife flush against the bone. Continue cutting in this manner from end to end until the breast comes away from the bone. Place boneless half breasts on cutting board and carve diagonally into thin slices. Arrange on serving platter.

To Carve a Chicken or Capon

Follow the same basic directions for turkey, but do not slice the meat from the drumsticks, thighs and breast into smaller pieces.

To Carve a Duck or Goose

Both ducks and geese differ anatomically from other poultry and contain considerably more fat and bone. Begin carving as you would for a turkey, but remove the legs from the body using a heavy chef's knife. This joint is located lower than on other poultry, actually under the breast. Since duck legs do not contain much meat, the thigh is often left attached.

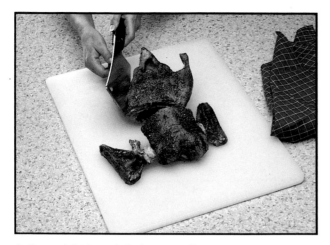

1. Roasted ducks and chickens are often cut up Chinese style. With a heavy cleaver, cut through back and breast to halve bird. Remove thighs and drumsticks at first joint; remove wings.

2. Cleave each half of bird the long way, then cut into inch-wide pieces. Use the cleaver to lift each half to serving platter, retaining original shape. Chop thighs, drumsticks and wings, and place on platter in original position.

INGREDIENT NOTES

BUTTER

Salt in butter acts as both a preservative and as a flavoring agent to mask rancidity. In addition, the salt content of butter varies from brand to brand, which creates inconsistencies in recipe testing. For such reasons, recipes in this book call for unsalted butter.

Unsalted butter, also known as sweet butter, is more perishable and therefore usually kept in the freezer section of your market. Unsalted butter is a pure product that tastes of fresh cream. It contains less water, and puts you in control of the amount of salt to be used in your cooking. If you substitute salted butter in any of the recipes in this book, reduce or eliminate the salt called for in the recipe.

GARLIC

There is no acceptable substitute for fresh garlic. Garlic that has been chopped, minced or pressed to release its volatile oils maintains a more characteristic taste and aroma. Furthermore, uncooked garlic is more pungent than cooked. Whole cloves cooked slowly over low heat take on a surprisingly sweet and nutty flavor. It is the method in which garlic is used, and not just the amount used, that determines its strength of flavor.

HERBS

Deciding whether to use fresh or dried herbs is like choosing between freshly ground coffee beans or freeze-dried coffee crystals. Although the latter might make an adequate substitute on occasion, it would never be mistaken for the former.

Fresh herbs add incomparable flavor and aroma to all foods; so much so that many people on restricted diets increase their use of culinary herbs to add life to otherwise bland foods. A sprig or two of your favorite herb tucked under poultry skin or inside the cavity of a bird before roasting will create a heady aroma as well as a real taste treat. Therefore, when cooking with herbs, the only decision between using fresh versus dried should be to use dried only when fresh isn't available.

As so many commonly used herbs thrive in poor soil outdoors or even in pots on a sunny windowsill, there is little reason for us not to grow our own. But fortunately for "brown thumbs," more markets are meeting the demand for fresh herbs by stocking organically or greenhouse grown herbs year around. If practicality demands that you use the dried variety, one teaspoon of dried leaf herbs is usually equivalent to one tablespoon of freshly chopped herbs. Since dried herbs have a short shelf life and tend to quickly lose their potency, it is important that you taste for seasonings as you proceed with any recipe.

To release maximum flavor from herbs, crush, chop or mince fresh ones and rub dried ones between your palms before using. Long cooking dissipates the flavor of herbs so it is usually best to add them during the last ten minutes of cooking if you want the herb flavor to predominate.

Herb bouquets are little bundles of aromatic herbs used to enliven stocks, stews, sauces and casseroles while cooking, and then removed before serving. Traditionally fresh herbs are just tied into a bouquet with a piece of kitchen twine, but I find that celery stalks add extra flavor as well as acting as a handy container. Use small cheesecloth squares if you are using a combination of dried and fresh ingredients.

BOUQUET GARNI (HERB BOUQUET)

1 celery stalk (or 1 (6-inch) square,
   double-thickness of prewashed cheesecloth)
3 parsley sprigs (preferably Italian parsley)
1 bay leaf
2 thyme sprigs or 1/2 teaspoon dried leaf thyme

Cut celery in half crosswise and press herbs into the concave interior, topping with the other celery half, concave-side down. Carefully secure the bundle with string. (Alternatively, place dried herbs in center of cheesecloth and gather corners up to form a pouch. Secure tightly with string.) Makes 1.

NUTS

A number of recipes in this book capitalize on the alluring flavors of various nuts. The oil in nuts will turn rancid over time, so many people prefer to store shelled nuts in the freezer. This may soften the meat, but it is easily remedied by toasting them in the oven.

Toasting nuts releases the fat contained in the nut and allows its flavoring and tenderizing properties to go into action, as well as developing their distinct fragrance.

To toast nuts: Preheat oven to 325F (165C). Spread nuts in a single layer on a baking sheet and bake 10 to 15 minutes, until golden-brown, shaking occasionally. Watch carefully, as smaller nut pieces cook quickly. Cool before adding to recipes.

OILS

Many oils can be used interchangeably at the discretion of the cook. However, for deep-frying, a light, flavorless vegetable oil is preferable. Those vegetable oils which hold up best under high heat are corn oil and peanut oil.

Olive oil imparts a mild flavor to salads and sautéed dishes. For a more pronounced flavor yet, use fruity olive oil, which is the heavier green oil from the first pressing of the olives, sometimes called extra-virgin olive oil. Fruity olive oil is best used for salads and marinades.

Aromatic sesame oil and hot chile oil do not withstand heat well, so they are usually added toward the end of a recipe and used primarily for seasonings. Flavored oils are great for marinades, basting, salads or pizza. Herb oil is a wonderful way to use up herb trimmings from your garden and make gifts for friends at the same time.

GARLIC OIL

2 cups olive oil or vegetable oil
10 to 12 garlic cloves, crushed with the side of a
   cleaver or knife

Combine ingredients in a clean glass jar or bottle with a narrow neck and tight-fitting lid or cork. Allow flavors to blend at least 48 hours at room temperature before using. Store in a cool, dry place. Makes about 1 pint.

Herb Oil

2 cups olive oil or vegetable oil

1 tarragon sprig or 1/2 teaspoon dried leaf
   tarragon

1 small dried red chile pepper

1 oregano sprig or 1 teaspoon dried leaf marjoram

1 thyme sprig or 1/2 teaspoon dried leaf thyme

Combine ingredients in a clean glass jar or bottle with a narrow neck and tight-fitting lid or cork. Allow flavors to blend at least 48 hours at room temperature before using. Store in a cool, dry place. Makes about 1 pint.

Pepper

Even the most spartan kitchen deserves a peppermill. Those of us who are true believers have at least two—one for black peppercorns and one for white. The aromatic oils that make pepper one of the world's most popular spices are released only when the peppercorn is freshly ground or crushed.

Salt

Common table salt contains additives to retard caking and make it flow freely. It is these additives that impart a slightly chemical aftertaste that can be detected in some dishes. In recipes where I feel the change of flavor is significant, I have specified the use of kosher salt. Kosher salt has large, coarse crystals that easily combine and blend into all foods. Because of the size of the crystals, substitute twice as much kosher salt as plain salt in any recipe. This two to one ratio has only to do with volume, not sodium content.

Rendered Chicken Fat & Cracklings

Rendered chicken fat, sometimes called *schmaltz,* can be used in lieu of oil or butter in sautés, sauces or gravies. Duck and goose fat is rendered in the same way.

Cracklings, or *grebenes,* are the crispy bits of skin that surface while rendering fat. These can be sprinkled with kosher salt for a snack, or reheated and used as you would bacon, in biscuits or corn bread, hash, chopped liver or pâtés, gravies, or tossed in salads or pasta dishes. Whenever you are preparing poultry, pull out the large pieces of fat from the tail end and any fatty skin, rinse with cold water and pat dry. Chop into pieces roughly 1/2-inch square and store in the freezer until you have accumulated about two pounds. Two pounds of solid chicken fat will render about one quart of fat.

To render fat, preheat oven to 275F (135C). Place frozen or thawed fat in a large, heavy flameproof pan and stir in 1/4 cup of warm water for each cup of fat. Cook over low heat until fat is partially melted.

Place pan in oven for about one hour, or until melted fat is clear, water has evaporated and the pieces of skin and fat solids floating on top are golden and sizzling. Remove from oven and lift off cracklings with a slotted spoon and drain on paper towels. Cool and store, covered, in refrigerator as long as five days.

Strain the rendered fat through a sieve lined with a paper coffee filter or a double thickness of cheesecloth and allow to cool. Cover and store in the refrigerator almost indefinitely.

Stocks

Anyone who has ever tried and failed to duplicate one of the intensely flavored soups or sauces served at better restaurants can usually remedy the situation by creating a rich, homemade stock to use as a base. Most restaurants keep a stock pot simmering at all times, but with a bit of forethought any of us can make a decent facsimile at home by saving bones and vegetable parings that might otherwise be discarded. It is the marrow and gelatin in the bones that give flavor and body to your stock, so simmer patiently to get the most for your efforts.

There are many brands of bouillon cubes and canned broths available, though they are poor substitutes—both dollar-wise and taste-wise—for the real thing. If you must use canned broth, add a little water to reduce the saltiness and simmer with a bit of onion, carrot, celery and parsley about 30 minutes, then strain before using in recipes.

The pot in which you cook stock should be narrow rather than wide so that all the ingredients steep in the liquid and the inevitable evaporation is kept to a minimum. There's no need to peel vegetables, as they will eventually be discarded, and their skins and stems lend additional color and flavor to your stock.

TURKEY GIBLET STOCK

To some, it wouldn't be a turkey dinner without Giblet Gravy (page 139). Here's how it all begins. (Reserve liver for another use, as it tends to make stock bitter.)

Turkey gizzard and heart
Turkey neck
1/2 small onion, coarsely chopped
1 small carrot, coarsely chopped
1 celery stalk, with leaves, coarsely chopped
A few parsley sprigs
4 peppercorns, cracked

Rinse giblets and neck with cold water. Place over medium heat in a 2-quart saucepan with vegetables and peppercorns. Cover with cold water and bring to a boil. Skim off any foam that rises to the top. Reduce heat to low and simmer 20 to 30 minutes. Strain stock through a fine sieve and reserve, skimming off any fat that rises to the top. Chop giblets and neck meat and reserve for Giblet Gravy or other uses. Makes about 1 quart.

CHICKEN STOCK

Making stock is an ideal project for a rainy Saturday and you'll happily reap the benefits in the weeks to come.

6 pounds chicken backs, necks, wing tips, feet, etc. with bits of meat and skin left on
3 carrots, coarsely chopped
2 onions, quartered
2 celery stalks with leaves, coarsely chopped
3 garlic cloves, unpeeled
1/2 bunch parsley, stems included
2 bay leaves
3 thyme sprigs or 1/2 teaspoon dried thyme leaves
1 teaspoon peppercorns, crushed

Place bones in a large stockpot and add enough cold water just to cover. Slowly bring to a simmer over medium heat, skimming off the fat and foam that rises to the top. After 30 minutes, add carrots, onion, celery, garlic, parsley, bay leaves, thyme and peppercorns. Partially cover and continue to simmer over low heat 3 hours, skimming occasionally. Discard bones and vegetables and strain stock through a fine sieve or colander lined with several layers of dampened cheesecloth. Cool to room temperature, then refrigerate at least 8 hours or overnight until the fat that has risen to the top of the container has solidified and can be lifted off and discarded. Stock can be kept in the refrigerator 2 to 3 days, or frozen up to 2 months.

Poultry Stock: Substitute pieces from turkey, duck or other poultry for chicken pieces.

TIP

Freeze stock in ice cube trays and small containers as quick-thawing flavor enhancers for sauce, soups and stews.

INTERNATIONAL

Each nation has its own poultry dishes, from rich and mild to hot and spicy. By exploring the cuisines of the world, you also encounter the mouthwatering versatility of poultry and game. Different ingredients and flavors have the ability to transform the humble bird into a world class meal.

Surprisingly, two dishes from dissimilar countries can share the same basic ingredients, yet still taste unique unto themselves. These national treasures are usually as delicious as they are educational. If, indeed, we are what we eat, there is no better way to bridge the international gap than by learning about the foods others consume.

One of the delights in researching this book was my personal "rediscovery" of Confit (page 30). Now that I have become accustomed to having rich, succulent precooked duck on hand at all times in my refrigerator, I doubt that I'll ever be without it again. Only a few hours of preparation yield a generous supply of tender duck to be used at your every whim (see suggestions for using Confit, page 31). Confit is quick and convenient—and the ultimate in fast food.

In this chapter I've selected a number of other favorite recipes, many of which may be unfamiliar to you. I hope that you'll expand your horizons and taste the tantalizing favorites from the rest of the world!

Chinese Lemon Chicken, page 26; Chicken Empanadas, page 28

CHINESE LEMON CHICKEN

There are many ways to prepare this dish, but this one is a favorite.

1 whole chicken breast, skinned,
    boned
Batter (recipe below)
Peanut oil or corn oil for deep-frying
Lemon Sauce (recipe below)
Lemon slices

BATTER:
1/2 cup all-purpose flour
1/4 cup cornstarch
1/2 teaspoon baking powder
1/4 teaspoon salt
3/4 cup water
1/2 teaspoon vegetable oil

LEMON SAUCE:
3 tablespoons fresh lemon juice
3 tablespoons sugar
1/2 cup water
1 teaspoon cornstarch mixed with 2
    tablespoons Chicken Stock (page
    23)

Rinse chicken with cold water and pat dry. Make Batter. Slice chicken into strips about 4" x 1/2". In a wok or other heavy pan, heat oil to 375F (190C) or until a 1-inch bread cube turns golden-brown in 50 seconds. Dip each piece of chicken into batter, allowing excess to drip off before sliding into hot oil. Deep-fry only 3 or 4 pieces of chicken at a time to prevent sticking. Deep-fry 4 to 5 minutes per batch, or until chicken floats freely close to surface and batter turns golden. Using a slotted spoon or Chinese strainer, remove chicken to paper towels to drain. Arrange chicken on serving platter. Cut each piece into 3 or 4 smaller pieces, but retain the shape of the original piece. Make sauce. Pour sauce over chicken. Garnish with lemon slices. Serve immediately. Makes 3 or 4 servings.

BATTER:
Mix batter ingredients together in a small bowl until smooth. Set aside.

LEMON SAUCE:
Mix lemon juice, sugar and water in a small saucepan. Bring to a boil. Stir in cornstarch mixture and cook, stirring, until mixture thickens.

RED-COOKED CHICKEN

Red-cooking gives the bird a rich chestnut color and faintly sweet flavor.

1 (4-1/2-lb.) roasting chicken
2 cups dark soy sauce
2 cups light soy sauce
1/2 cup Chinese rice wine, dry sherry
    or vermouth
1/2 cup packed light-brown sugar
1 tablespoon Szechuan peppercorns,
    roasted
1 whole star anise
1/2 teaspoon fennel seeds
2 gingerroot slices, crushed with the
    side of a heavy knife or cleaver
2 cups Chicken Stock (page 23)
2 tablespoons sesame oil
Cilantro sprigs

Rinse chicken with cold water and pat dry. In a large pot or wok, bring soy sauces, wine, brown sugar, peppercorns, anise, fennel, gingerroot and stock to a boil, then reduce to a simmer. Add chicken. Simmer, covered, 25 minutes. Turn off heat and let chicken steep, covered, 1 hour. Remove chicken from pot and drain until surface of skin is dry. The braising liquid can be refrigerated and reused, if desired. Rub chicken with sesame oil. Chop it Chinese-style into bite-size pieces, if desired. Arrange on a large oval serving platter; garnish with cilantro. Makes 4 to 6 servings.

PETTO DI TACCHINO ALLA BOLOGNESE

You'll love this with a tossed green salad and crusty Italian bread.

1 cup Simple Tomato Sauce (recipe below)
2 pounds boneless turkey breast, sliced 1 inch thick, pounded lightly
1 cup all-purpose flour
Salt and freshly ground pepper to taste
3 tablespoons unsalted butter
2 tablespoons olive oil
1 cup dry Marsala wine or sherry
1/2 cup whipping cream
1/4 pound prosciutto, sliced paper thin
1/2 cup freshly grated Parmesan cheese

SIMPLE TOMATO SAUCE:
2 pounds plum tomatoes or 1 can (28-oz.) Italian-style tomatoes
2 tablespoons olive oil
Salt and freshly ground pepper to taste

Make sauce. Rinse turkey with cold water and pat dry. Flour turkey slices lightly and season with salt and pepper. In a large heavy skillet, melt butter with oil. When butter foams, add turkey; sauté until golden on both sides. Transfer turkey to a warm plate. Pour Marsala into skillet and deglaze, scraping with a wooden spoon to remove any brown bits which cling to the bottom. When wine is reduced by half, add cream and mix until it bubbles. Stir in tomato sauce and simmer 5 minutes. Put a slice of prosciutto and 2 tablespoons Parmesan cheese over each turkey slice and arrange in a single layer in skillet. Cover and simmer 5 minutes or until cheese is melted. Transfer meat to a warm serving platter, spoon sauce over and serve immediately. Makes 6 to 8 servings.

SIMPLE TOMATO SAUCE:
Put tomatoes through a food mill. Heat oil in a medium-size saucepan. Add tomatoes. Season with salt and pepper. Cook, uncovered, 20 to 25 minutes, until thickened.

TANDOORI CHICKEN

This Indian specialty is traditionally cooked in a clay oven called a tandoor, *which simultaneously bakes, roasts and grills. The American home cook can achieve delicious results by using the same classic marinade and roasting in a conventional oven. Because this dish is low in calories and cholesterol, it is ideal for today's cook.*

Tandoori Marinade (recipe below)
1 (3-1/2-lb.) chicken, halved
3 tablespoons unsalted butter, melted

TANDOORI MARINADE:
1 cup plain yogurt
1/2 cup fresh lemon juice
1 tablespoon paprika
1 tablespoon minced garlic
1 tablespoon minced gingerroot
1-1/2 teaspoons ground cumin
1-1/2 teaspoons red (cayenne) pepper
1 teaspoon ground turmeric
1/2 teaspoon ground cardamom
Salt and freshly ground pepper to taste

Make marinade. Remove chicken skin and discard or reserve for other uses. Rinse chicken with cold water and pat dry. Make diagonal slashes 1/2 inch deep and 1 inch apart in the meat. Coat all sides of chicken with marinade, working it into the slashes; place in a large glass or ceramic dish. Cover and marinate in the refrigerator at least 4 hours or overnight. Remove from refrigerator 1 hour before roasting. Preheat oven to 450F (230C). Brush melted butter over the marinade clinging to chicken and place on a rack in a roasting pan. Roast 30 minutes, or until meat is cooked through. Makes 4 servings.

TANDOORI MARINADE:
Combine all ingredients together in a small bowl.

Chicken Empañadas

This updated version of savory Mexican turnovers uses a simplified pastry that is baked rather than fried. Make miniature empañadas for cocktail parties!

Cream Cheese Pastry (recipe below)
Chicken Filling (recipe below)
Large egg, lightly beaten

CREAM CHEESE PASTRY:
2 cups all-purpose flour
2 (3-oz.) packages cream cheese
1 cup unsalted butter

CHICKEN FILLING:
1/3 cup raisins
3 tablespoons vegetable oil
2/3 cup minced onion
1 pound boneless, skinned chicken, diced
3 tablespoons pine nuts, toasted
3 tablespoons chopped green olives
3 to 4 chili pequins, crushed*
1-1/3 teaspoons salt
Pinch of cinnamon

Make pastry. Preheat oven to 375F (190C). Make filling. Roll dough 1/8 inch thick on a floured surface and cut with a 5- or 6-inch round cutter. Place one-sixth of filling on one-half of each circle and brush edges with water. Fold rounds in half, shaping into crescents, and press edges together with the tines of a fork. Line a baking sheet with parchment paper. Lay crescents on prepared baking sheet, brush with egg and bake 30 minutes, until golden-brown. Makes 6 to 8 empañadas.

CREAM CHEESE PASTRY:
Combine ingredients with a fork, or in a food processor fitted with the metal blade, until mixture forms a ball. Wrap in waxed paper and refrigerate 1 hour while preparing chicken filling.

CHICKEN FILLING:
Cover raisins with 1 cup boiling water 10 minutes, then drain. Set aside. Heat oil in a medium-size skillet. Add onion; sauté until softened but not browned, about 5 minutes. Stir in chicken and remaining ingredients. Sauté over medium heat 5 minutes or until chicken is no longer pink. Remove from heat and cool thoroughly.

*Chili pequins are the very small and very hot red chilies usually found dried in Hispanic or Asian markets.

Chinese Poached Chicken

Serve this moist and delicious entree with boiled Chinese noodles or steamed rice and sautéed snow peas with mushrooms and water chestnuts.

1 (3-lb.) chicken
3/4 cup light soy sauce
1/4 cup dry vermouth or dry sherry
1/4 cup water
4 green onions, coarsely chopped
3 garlic cloves, bruised
1 tablespoon sugar
3 quarter-size gingerroot slices, peeled, crushed
1 teaspoon five-spice powder
A few cilantro sprigs

Rinse chicken with cold water. Place the chicken, breast-side down, in a wok or a 5-quart dutch oven. In a medium-size bowl, combine all the other ingredients and pour over the chicken. Cover and bring the liquid to a simmer over medium heat. Reduce heat to medium-low to maintain the simmer; cook, covered, 30 minutes. Turn the chicken breast-side up, re-cover and simmer 30 minutes more, or until chicken is tender. Remove chicken from wok or pot and place on a serving platter. Discard poaching liquid and vegetables. Garnish with cilantro. Makes 4 servings.

Braised Chicken Drumsticks On Romaine Lettuce

Lettuce makes an unusual and tasty warm vegetable in this Chinese-style dish.

10 chicken drumsticks
2 tablespoons dry white wine or
    vermouth
3 tablespoons light soy sauce
4 cups Chicken Stock (page 23)
2 teaspoons red wine vinegar
1/2 teaspoon salt
2 green onions, cut into
    1-1/2-inch-long pieces
1 (1-inch) piece peeled gingerroot,
    crushed with side of a heavy knife
    or cleaver
4 cups vegetable oil
5 teaspoons sugar
2 teaspoons cornstarch mixed with 4
    teaspoons water
1 small head romaine lettuce, cut into
    1/4-inch strips

Rinse drumsticks in cold water and pat dry. In a large bowl, combine 1 tablespoon of wine with soy sauce. Add drumsticks and marinate 30 minutes. Remove drumsticks and drain, discarding the marinade. In a separate bowl, combine Chicken Stock, remaining wine, vinegar, salt, green onions and gingerroot. Set aside. Heat oil in a wok or large skillet over medium heat until hot. Add drumsticks, a few at a time, if necessary, and fry until golden brown, about 10 minutes. Remove drumsticks and drain. Empty all but 2-1/2 tablespoons of oil into a bowl and set aside.

Heat remaining oil in the wok over medium heat just until warm. Add sugar and stir constantly until the mixture turns golden. Immediately add the stock mixture and drumsticks. Bring to a boil, then reduce heat to low and simmer 30 minutes. Remove green onions and gingerroot. Stir in cornstarch mixture. Increase heat to medium and cook, stirring constantly, until sauce thickens and coats drumsticks. In another wok or large skillet, heat reserved oil over high heat until it reaches 375F (190C) or until a 1-inch bread cube turns golden brown in 50 seconds. Add lettuce strips and deep-fry until they darken, about 5 seconds. Remove from oil, drain and heap in center of a platter. Arrange drumsticks in a circle around lettuce; pour remaining sauce over drumsticks and serve. Makes 4 to 6 servings.

DUCK CONFIT

Confits consist of meat which has been salted and seasoned, cooked and preserved in fat until needed.
This recipes calls for only one duck, but you should really make as much as your refrigerator space will allow. Once you enjoy the benefits of having confit on hand, you'll start saving fat in the freezer so you'll always have enough for your next batch.

1 duck (about 5-lbs.), quartered, or 2 pairs of duck legs with thighs attached
1/2 cup kosher salt
2 bay leaves, crumbled
3 tablespoons fresh herbs, such as thyme and/or marjoram, or 1 tablespoon dried leaf herbs
1 garlic clove, minced
1 tablespoon peppercorns, crushed
6 to 8 cups solid (unrendered) duck, goose or chicken fat, or pork leaf lard from your butcher, or a combination thereof

Rinse duck in cold water and pat dry. Pull out all loose fat from cavity and reserve. Reserve duck neck, liver and giblets for other uses. In a small bowl, mix together salt, herbs, garlic and peppercorns. Rub the duck pieces well with this mixture, place in a large glass or stainless steel bowl and cover with any remaining salt mixture. Cover with plastic wrap and cure in the refrigerator 36 to 48 hours.

Remove the duck from the salt cure and wipe free of salt mixture with a paper towel. Render the fat in a large deep pan that will hold the duck pieces in one layer, discarding any bits that do not melt. Place the duck pieces snugly inside the pan so that they are completely covered by hot fat. Simmer very gently until the duck is quite tender when pierced with a skewer, 1 to 1-1/2 hours. Remove duck from fat with a slotted spoon and let cool. Carefully pour the fat through a fine sieve once or twice until clear and set aside or refrigerate briefly until the fat solidifies and rises to the top. Carefully lift out the fat with a slotted spoon, leaving the juices and any other debris behind. (Juices can be saved for stock.) Reheat the solidified fat and strain once again to remove any impurities. Pack the duck pieces in a sterile 1-1/2- to 2-quart heatproof glass or stoneware jug glazed on the inside only. (The containers should be taller than they are wide, yet wide enough to hold the pieces of duck in single layers, so that you will need less fat to cover the meat.) Pour the melted and strained fat over the duck pieces until they are completely covered, with at least a 1-inch layer of fat on the top. Cool to room temperature and then cover and refrigerate at least 2 weeks or as long as 3 months. Do not freeze, as this would inhibit the ripening process and dry out the meat.

To use Confit, set the jar in a warm room or water bath until the fat has softened, about 4 hours. Remove as many pieces as you need, taking care that the remaining pieces are still completely sealed in fat (cover with peanut oil at this point, if necessary). Once a jar of confit has been opened like this, it is best to use the remainder within 7 days. Confit should always be reheated before serving, even when it will be served cold or at room temperature. To reheat, remove all but a tablespoon of the fat from the duck pieces and roast in a pan in a 400F (205C) oven 10 to 15 minutes to crisp the skin and render out excess fat. Makes 2 servings.

USES FOR CONFIT:

Slices or chunks can be used in any recipes calling for cooked duck, such as salads or pizzas.

Small pieces of Confit are a wonderful addition to soups and vegetables, such as cabbage or green beans.

Large pieces of Confit are ideal for cassoulet.

Whole pieces of roasted Confit are excellent by themselves, or served with thin-sliced potatoes that have been fried in Confit fat until crisp.

VARIATIONS

Goose Confit: Use an 8- to 10-pound goose cut into 8 to 10 pieces. Double the amount of salt, herbs and peppercorns, and add 12 lightly crushed juniper berries. Cure 24 hours in the refrigerator. Cook 2 to 2-1/2 hours.

Turkey Confit: Use a 10- to 12-pound turkey cut into 8 pieces. Double the amount of salt, herbs and peppercorns. Cure 18 to 24 hours in the refrigerator. Cook 1 to 1-1/2 hours.

HONEY BAKED GAME HENS

Chinese in origin, this recipe works equally well with a plump chicken.

6 Cornish game hens
1 tablespoon five-spice powder
1-1/2 tablespoons plum sauce
3 tablespoons brown bean sauce
2-1/2 tablespoons hoisin sauce
2 tablespoons dry sherry
1/3 cup light soy sauce
1/3 cup honey
2 tablespoons water
1 bunch cilantro

Rinse game hens with cold water and pat dry. Rub cavities with five-spice powder. In a small bowl, mix plum, bean and hoisin sauces and sherry. Rub cavities with half of sauce. Rub skins with remaining sauce. Cover with plastic wrap and refrigerate overnight. Preheat oven to 350F (175C). Rub hens to even out marinade; place them in a shallow roasting pan. In a small bowl, mix soy sauce, honey and water. Roast, back-side up, 25 minutes, brushing with half of honey mixture after 15 minutes. Turn breast-side up and roast another 20 minutes, brushing with remaining sauce after 10 minutes. Skin should be golden-brown and juices should be clear when hen is pierced with a fork. Remove from oven and rest 10 to 15 minutes. Garnish with cilantro sprigs. Makes 6 servings.

CIRCASSIAN CHICKEN

I learned how to prepare this traditional cold buffet dish while visiting Turkey. Because it is so rich, a crisp green salad and dinner rolls are the only accompaniments needed.

2 (2-1/2- to 3-lb.) chickens, quartered
2 onions, quartered
2 carrots, halved
1 tablespoon salt
4 firm white bread slices, crusts removed
3 cups walnuts (about 1-1/2 lbs.)
2 onions, coarsely chopped
Salt and freshly ground pepper to taste
Lettuce leaves, for garnish
1/4 cup walnut oil or vegetable oil
1 tablespoon sweet Hungarian paprika

Place chickens in a 5- or 6-quart pan with quartered onions, carrots and salt. Add water to cover and bring to a boil over medium heat. Reduce heat to low and simmer, skimming the surface occasionally, until chickens are tender, about 40 minutes. Remove vegetables with a slotted spoon and discard. Transfer chicken pieces to a large pan and cool. Strain stock through a fine sieve and cool to room temperature. Discard fat that rises to the top. Skin and bone chickens. Slice or tear meat into strips and set aside in a medium-size bowl. Soak bread slices in 2/3 cup of the reserved stock about 1 minute and squeeze dry; reserve. Finely chop walnuts in several batches in a food processor fitted with the metal blade. Return all nuts to processor and add bread and chopped onions. Process to a thick paste. With the motor running, pour in 1-1/2 cups of the reserved stock to make a thick and creamy sauce. Adjust seasonings. Line a platter with lettuce. Mix half of walnut sauce with reserved chicken pieces; arrange on lettuce-lined platter. Pour the remaining sauce over the top. In a small pan over low heat, gently warm the oil and whisk in paprika. Remove from heat and allow to cool slightly. Use the back of a spoon to decoratively make small indentations on the surface of the walnut sauce; fill with paprika oil. Serve slightly chilled or at room temperature. Makes 8 servings.

SHREDDED CHICKEN IN SZECHUAN SAUCE

Full of wonderful flavors, this will be appreciated by lovers of spicy foods.

2 chicken drumsticks and thighs
1 tablespoon Szechuan peppercorns
2 tablespoons peanut oil
2 garlic cloves, minced
1/2 teaspoon minced gingerroot
1/4 cup Chicken Stock (page 23)
1 teaspoon dark soy sauce
1 teaspoon medium-dry sherry or vermouth
Pinch of sugar
1-1/2 teaspoons white distilled vinegar
2 teaspoons cornstarch mixed with 1 tablespoon water

Rinse chicken with cold water. Steam chicken in a steamer over boiling water about 30 minutes or until tender. Cool, discard skin and bones, remove meat and shred. Cool to room temperature. In a wok or skillet over medium-high heat, roast peppercorns until fragrant, then pulverize in a mini food processor, mortar or with the handle of a cleaver. Heat wok over medium-high heat; add oil, garlic and gingerroot. Sauté until fragrant, about 30 seconds. Add peppercorns, stock, soy sauce, sherry, sugar and vinegar. When sauce boils, slowly stir in cornstarch mixture to lightly thicken sauce. Cool slightly. Gently toss with chicken before serving. Makes 2 or 3 servings.

TEA SMOKED DUCK

Use this same Chinese technique for chicken or game birds. Do not attempt this dish unless you have a well ventilated kitchen and a heavy pot that can be tightly sealed. A large wok or roasting pan is ideal. You will also need some heavy-duty foil, two empty tuna cans, tops and bottoms removed, and a rack that will fit inside the wok or pan.

1 (4-1/2- to 5-lb.) duck
1 tablespoon Szechuan peppercorns
2 tablespoons kosher salt
1/4 cup black tea leaves
1/4 cup packed brown sugar
1 tablespoon fennel seeds
2 pieces whole star anise
1 cinnamon stick
1/4 cup long-grain rice
1 tablespoon sesame oil

Rinse duck with cold water and pat dry. Place peppercorns in a wok or small heavy skillet and roast over low heat, shaking constantly to prevent sticking. When peppercorns begin to smoke, transfer to a mini food processor or mortar and grind to a fine powder. Add salt to wok and stir over low heat with a wooden spoon until the salt turns light-brown in color. Combine salt and peppercorns and rub all over duck. Cover tightly with plastic wrap and store overnight in refrigerator. Fill a large wok or roasting pan that can be tightly sealed with about 2 inches of water. Place 2 empty cans in pan and place rack on top of them. Cover and bring the water to a boil. Open lid and place duck on rack. Cover again and steam 1-1/2 hours, checking water level periodically and replacing liquid, if necessary. Remove duck on its rack and set aside. Wash and dry the wok and line with a few layers of heavy-duty foil. Make sure foil is as flat and smooth as possible to allow it to conduct heat. Place tea, brown sugar, fennel, anise, cinnamon and rice in center of pan. Add the 2 tin cans and replace duck. Cover the wok, sealing the edges as tightly as possible with foil strips. Place tightly sealed wok over medium heat. Look and sniff for signs of smoke, then reduce heat and smoke duck 15 minutes. Turn off heat and let smoke settle. Remove duck, cool slightly and brush with sesame oil. Chop duck into bite-size pieces. Serve immediately or cover and store in the refrigerator several days. (The flavor will intensify during storage.) Makes 2 or 3 servings.

VARIATION

Heat 6 cups peanut oil or corn oil in a wok to 375F (190C). Gently lower smoked duck, breast-side down and head first, into oil. Support the duck underneath with a large strainer and ladle hot oil over the exposed top. After 3 minutes, turn duck and cook 2 minutes more. Drain oil from duck, cool and cut into bite-size pieces. Serve immediately.

ENCHILADAS SUIZAS

This recipe comes from Marge Poore, a San Francisco Bay Area cooking teacher who specializes in the cuisines of Mexico.

Salsa Verde (recipe below)
Vegetable oil
12 corn tortillas
2 cups shredded cooked chicken,
    moistened with a little of the Salsa
    Verde
1/2 cup chopped green onions
1 cup dairy sour cream
2 tablespoons Chicken Stock (page
    23) or milk
8 ounces Jack cheese, shredded

SALSA VERDE:

10 tomatillos or 1 (13-oz.) can
    tomatillos
6 poblano chiles, roasted, peeled and
    seeds removed
2 serrano chiles, minced
3 cilantro sprigs
1/2 onion, chopped
1 garlic clove, minced
2 tablespoons vegetable oil
Sugar
Salt and freshly ground pepper to taste

Make Salsa Verde. Preheat oven to 325F (165C). Lightly oil a 13" x 9" baking dish. Heat 1 inch of oil in a medium-size skillet over medium heat. Soften tortillas 1 at a time in hot oil. Drain between double sheets of paper towels and keep warm while softening remaining tortillas. Dip each tortilla in warm salsa. Place some shredded chicken mixture on each tortilla and roll. Place seam-side down in prepared baking dish. When all are filled and rolled, pour remaining salsa over all and top with green onions. Thin the sour cream with stock or milk and pour over the enchiladas. Sprinkle with cheese and bake 15 to 20 minutes, or until heated through and bubbly. Makes 6 servings.

SALSA VERDE:

Remove and discard husks from tomatillos, rinse and coarsely chop. Cook in a medium-size saucepan 5 to 8 minutes, until tender. If using canned tomatillos, drain, rinse with cold water and drain again. Place tomatillos in a blender or food processor fitted with the metal blade with chiles, cilantro, onion and garlic and puree. Heat oil in heavy pan over medium-high heat; stir in the puree. Add a dash of sugar, salt and pepper to taste and cook about 5 minutes, until reduced and thickened slightly.

CHICKEN SATAY WITH PEANUT SAUCE

Serve this popular appetizer, a specialty of Southeast Asia, also as an entree. Make plenty, as they're sure to be eaten quickly.

4 chicken breast halves, skinned, boned
Marinade (recipe below)
Peanut Sauce (recipe below) (optional)

MARINADE:
2 garlic cloves, minced
2 gingerroot slices, crushed with side of a knife or cleaver
3 tablespoons dry vermouth
3 tablespoons peanut oil
2 tablespoons oyster sauce
2 tablespoons soy sauce
2 tablespoons chili sauce
1 tablespoon Hoisin sauce
1 tablespoon sesame oil
1 tablespoon hot pepper sauce
1-1/2 teaspoons sugar
1/2 teaspoon salt
1/2 teaspoon freshly ground black pepper
1 tablespoon cornstarch mixed with 1 tablespoon water
1/4 cup peanut butter mixed with 1/3 cup warm water

PEANUT SAUCE:
2 tablespoons peanut oil
1 small onion, minced
2 garlic cloves, minced
1 (18-oz.) jar crunchy peanut butter
2 tablespoons soy sauce
1 teaspoon red (cayenne) pepper
About 1 cup coconut milk
1/4 cup finely chopped cilantro

Soak 40 (6-inch) bamboo skewers in water at least 1 hour to prevent burning. Rinse chicken with cold water and pat dry. Slice meat across the grain into strips about 4 inches long, 1-1/2 inches wide and 1/4 inch thick. Thread chicken strips on skewers and place in a large glass or ceramic dish. Make marinade; pour over skewered chicken. Cover and marinate 1 hour at room temperature or 2 hours in the refrigerator. Meanwhile make Peanut Sauce, if desired.

Preheat gas grill or ignite charcoal and burn until flame is gone and charcoal is covered with a uniform gray ash. Drain chicken, reserving marinade. Grill chicken, 3 inches above heat, 3 to 5 minutes, brushing occasionally with remaining marinade. Serve plain or with Peanut Sauce for dipping. Makes 10 appetizer servings.

MARINADE:
Combine all ingredients in a medium-size bowl.

PEANUT SAUCE:
Heat oil in a medium-size skillet over medium-low heat. Add onion and garlic; sauté until softened but not browned. Stir in peanut butter, soy sauce and cayenne; simmer about 10 minutes, stirring occasionally. When oil begins to separate from mixture, gradually stir in 1 cup coconut milk. Remove from heat and stir in cilantro. Sauce may be served warm or at room temperature. If made ahead and chilled, sauce may need to be thinned with a bit more coconut milk.

American Classics

Americans have savored the pleasures of poultry for as long as history has been recorded. From the natives and immigrants celebrating the first Thanksgiving, to the family dinners immortalized by Norman Rockwell, nothing typifies America more than a festive meal featuring its native bird, the turkey.

Through good times and bad, through prosperity and Depression, poultry has been a mainstay of the American diet. Not too many years ago a Sunday dinner was often one of the chickens from the family farm. Now, however, there are entire generations who have only eaten chicken from the supermarket!

The diverse ethnic backgrounds that form our collective culture contribute to the distinct flavors so evident in American classics. These cultural differences have also affected the evolution of various regional specialties. A walk across America is only as far away as your kitchen, so take the time to make your friends and family an all-American meal next Sunday!

Missouri Fried Chicken, page 38; Make-ahead Mashed Potatoes, page 148; Buttermilk Biscuits, page 132

MISSOURI FRIED CHICKEN

Chicken the way my Grandma Grace always made it, and it's still my favorite!

1 (4-lb.) chicken, cut up (page 13)
2 cups buttermilk
2 cups all-purpose flour
2 tablespoons kosher salt
1 tablespoon coarsely ground pepper
Vegetable oil or shortening for frying

Rinse chicken in cold water, pat dry and place in a large bowl. Pour buttermilk over chicken, cover with plastic wrap and refrigerate at least 4 hours or up to 48 hours. Bring chicken back to room temperature before proceeding with recipe. Drain chicken. Place flour, salt and pepper in a paper or plastic bag and toss chicken pieces, one or two at a time, until very well coated. Set aside on a rack to dry. In a large skillet or wok over high heat, heat 2 inches of oil to 375F (190C) or until a 1-inch bread cube turns golden-brown in 50 seconds. Add chicken pieces, without crowding. (Cook in 2 batches, if necessary.) When temperature returns to 375F (190C), reduce heat to medium. Cook until golden-brown on both sides, about 5 minutes for white meat and 15 minutes for dark pieces. Increase heat to medium-high and finish browning, about 5 minutes more. Drain well before serving. Makes 4 servings.

BRUNSWICK STEW

An adaptation of a popular southern dish, this stew is said to have originated in Brunswick County, Virginia. The original recipe called for squirrel, but as wild game became scarce, chicken was substituted.

1 (4- to 5-lb.) chicken, cut into
   serving pieces
5 bacon slices
2 cups corn cut from 6 medium-size
   ears or 1 (10-oz.) package frozen
   whole-kernel corn, thawed
2 cups fresh lima beans or 1 (10-oz.)
   package frozen lima beans, thawed
3 large tomatoes, peeled, chopped or 1
   (14-1/2-oz.) can Italian plum
   tomatoes, drained, chopped
2 medium-size russet potatoes, cut in
   1-inch cubes
1 large onion, coarsely chopped
2 teaspoons salt
Freshly ground pepper to taste
2 cups Chicken Stock (page 23)

Preheat oven to 325F (165C). Rinse chicken in cold water and pat dry. Cut bacon in small pieces and fry in a large skillet until crisp. Remove with a slotted spoon and set aside. In the same skillet, brown chicken pieces in bacon fat until a rich mahogany color. Discard cooking fat. Place chicken in a 5-quart casserole dish, top with vegetables, seasonings, Chicken Stock and reserved bacon. Cover and bake 1 hour, or until chicken is tender and falls from the bone. Makes 6 servings.

BUFFALO CHICKEN WINGS

This spicy appetizer originated at the Anchor Bar in Buffalo, New York when the owner received a large order of chicken wings from her supplier. The rest, as they say, is history. Tradition dictates that these be served with crisp celery sticks and a creamy blue cheese dressing to "cool the fire."

Blue Cheese Dressing (recipe below)
24 whole chicken wings (about 4 pounds)
Salt and freshly ground pepper to taste
4 cups peanut oil or other vegetable oil
1/4 cup unsalted butter
2 to 5 tablespoons (1 (2-1/2-oz.) bottle) Frank's Louisiana Red Hot Sauce or other hot-pepper sauce
1 tablespoon white vinegar
Celery sticks

BLUE CHEESE DRESSING:
1/2 cup dairy sour cream
1/2 cup Basic Mayonnaise (page 141)
2 tablespoons chopped green onion
2 garlic cloves, minced
1 tablespoon white wine vinegar
1/4 pound blue cheese, crumbled

Make dressing; refrigerate. Rinse wings in cold water and pat dry. Cut off small pointed tip of each wing and reserve for stock or another use. Cut the main wing bone and second wing bone at the joint so you end up with 24 drumettes as well as 24 flat wing portions. Season with salt and pepper. In a deep-fat fryer, wok or heavy pot, heat oil to 375F (190C) or until a 1-inch bread cube turns golden-brown in 50 seconds. Place about 1/3 of the wings in the oil and cook until golden-brown and crisp, about 10 minutes. Remove from oil and drain well. Cook the remaining chicken wings in the same manner. Melt butter in a small saucepan and add hot sauce and vinegar. Pour over chicken wings or serve on the side as a dipping sauce. Serve dressing as a dipping sauce for chicken and celery. Makes 4 to 6 servings.

BLUE CHEESE DRESSING:
Combine all ingredients in a medium-size bowl. Makes 1-1/2 cups.

CLUB SANDWICH

Now served in hotels and restaurants all over the world, this is an American classic. Some may scorn a "triple-decker," but this version is traditional as well as delicious.

3 slices good-quality, thinly sliced white bread (crusts removed if desired)
1 tablespoon unsalted butter, softened
1 medium-size leaf of green leaf lettuce
3 tablespoons Basic Mayonnaise (page 141)
3 roasted chicken breast slices
2 tomato slices
Salt and freshly ground pepper to taste
2 bacon slices, crisp-cooked, drained

Toast bread. While the toast slices are still warm, spread 1 side of each with butter. Place lettuce on 1 buttered slice, then top with all the chicken and 1 tablespoon of the mayonnaise. Cover with another piece of toast and 1 tablespoon of mayonnaise, then tomato, salt and pepper and bacon. Spread remaining mayonnaise on the remaining buttered toast slice and place on top to finish the sandwich. Secure with wooden picks, if desired, and cut into halves or quarters before serving. Makes 1 serving.

BATTER FRIED CHICKEN

Partially cooking chicken before deep-frying ensures moist, fully cooked meat and a light, crispy crust.

1 (3-1/2-lb.) chicken, cut up, skinned
1 cup all-purpose flour
1 teaspoon salt
1/2 teaspoon paprika
1/4 teaspoon freshly ground pepper
1 large egg
About 1/2 cup milk
2 cups Chicken Stock (page 23)
All-purpose flour for dredging
About 2 quarts vegetable oil for
   deep-frying

Rinse chicken with cold water and pat dry. In a small bowl or a food processor, mix flour, salt, paprika, pepper, egg and 1/2 cup milk until thoroughly blended. Cover and set aside 1 hour. Meanwhile, bring stock to a boil over medium heat in a pan large enough to hold chicken pieces in a single layer. Reduce heat to low, add chicken, cover and simmer 20 minutes. Remove chicken and pat dry. Reserve stock for other uses. Test consistency of batter; if it seems too thick, whisk in more milk. (Batter should not be much thicker than heavy cream.) In an electric deep-fryer or a large heavy kettle, heat oil to 350F (175C) or until a 1-inch bread cube turns golden-brown in 1 minute. Dust a few chicken pieces with flour. Using tongs, dip floured chicken into batter, allowing excess to drip off, and then completely submerge in hot oil, without crowding pieces, 7 to 10 minutes, or until chicken is golden-brown. Remove chicken with tongs and drain on paper towels. Let oil return to 350F (175C) before frying remaining pieces of chicken in the same manner. Makes 4 servings.

VARIATION
For an extra crunchy exterior, substitute 1/2 cup cornmeal for half of the flour in the batter.

COBB SALAD

This ever-popular composed salad was created in 1936 by the president of the Brown Derby Restaurant in Hollywood. Hooray for Bob Cobb!

French Dressing Derby (recipe below)
1/2 head iceberg lettuce
1/2 head romaine lettuce
1/2 bunch watercress
1 small bunch curly endive
2 tablespoons minced chives
2 medium-size tomatoes, peeled,
   seeded and diced
2 chicken breast halves, cooked,
   skinned, boned, chilled and diced
6 bacon slices, crisp-cooked, diced
1 large avocado, diced
3 hard-cooked eggs, diced
1/2 cup (about 2 oz.) crumbled
   Roquefort cheese

FRENCH DRESSING DERBY:

1/2 cup red wine vinegar
1 tablespoon lemon juice
1-1/2 teaspoons freshly ground pepper
1 teaspoon salt
1/2 teaspoon sugar
1/2 teaspoon dry mustard
1 teaspoon Worcestershire sauce
1 garlic clove, minced
3/4 cup olive oil
3/4 cup vegetable oil

Make dressing; refrigerate. Finely chop lettuces, watercress and endive by hand or in a food processor. Place in a large wide bowl or 6 individual wide shallow bowls. Sprinkle with chives. Arrange a row each of tomatoes, chicken, bacon, avocado, eggs and cheese across top of greens. If made an hour or so in advance, cover and refrigerate, but allow time for salad to sit at room temperature 15 minutes before serving. To serve, bring salad to the table, toss with 1/2 cup dressing and pass remaining dressing separately. Or pass dressing for individual salads. Makes 6 servings.

FRENCH DRESSING DERBY:

Combine vinegar, lemon juice, pepper, salt, sugar, mustard, Worcestershire sauce and garlic. Whisk in oils and refrigerate. Bring to room temperature before serving. Makes about 2 cups.

VARIATION

At my favorite neighborhood restaurant in San Francisco, Cafe For All Seasons, Chef Donna Katzl makes a wonderful Cobb Salad Sandwich, placing a grilled chicken breast, Roquefort cheese, bacon, avocado, tomatoes, mixed lettuces and mayonnaise between 2 slices of toasted homemade bread. Heavenly!

TIP

To prevent discoloration, rinse cut up avocado in bowl of cool water, then lift out, drain and cover with plastic wrap until serving time.

On following pages: Classic Roast Turkey, page 45 with Sausage & Apple Stuffing, page 134; Cranberry Salsa, page 143; Buttermilk Biscuits, page 132

HOLIDAY ROAST GOOSE

Roasting a goose at two temperatures makes for crisper skin and moist, tender meat. The addition of aromatic fruit and vegetables contributes to a more flavorful gravy.

1 (8- to 10-lb.) goose
Salt and freshly ground pepper to taste
1 small onion, coarsely chopped
3/4 pound tart apples, coarsely
    chopped
2 fresh thyme sprigs or 1-1/2
    teaspoons dried leaf thyme
1/4 cup coarsely chopped carrot
1/4 cup coarsely chopped celery
Giblet Gravy (page 139) (optional)

Preheat oven to 400F (205C). Remove neck and giblets from goose and reserve for Giblet Gravy, if desired. Remove excess fat from body cavity and neck skin and reserve for confit or other uses. Rinse goose with cold water and pat dry. Season inside and out with salt and pepper. Stuff cavity with apples and thyme and truss, if desired. Place goose, breast-side up, on a rack in a large roasting pan. Prick the skin all over with a sharp skewer or fork to allow fat to escape during cooking. Roast 1 hour, removing accumulated fat from the roasting pan with a bulb baster 2 or 3 times. Reduce heat to 325F (165C) and roast 1 hour more. Scatter vegetables in the pan and roast an additional 30 minutes, or until a meat thermometer inserted into the thigh registers 185F (85C) and juices run clear when leg is pierced with a fork. Rest 20 to 30 minutes before carving. Serve with Giblet Gravy, if desired. Makes 8 servings.

CRISPY ROAST CHICKEN

Nothing could be easier or more delicious. Go ahead and roast two chickens at once so you can enjoy leftovers the next day.

1 (3-1/2-lb.) chicken
1 lemon, halved
Salt and freshly ground pepper to taste
1 small onion, quartered
About 1/2 cup fresh herbs such as
    parsley, sage, thyme, marjoram or a
    combination
2 tablespoons unsalted butter, or
    Compound Butter (pages 136 to
    137), softened, or 2 tablespoons
    olive oil
Paprika
Chicken au Jus (page 139) (optional)

Preheat oven to 400F (205C). Remove fat, neck, gizzards and liver from chicken and reserve for other uses. Rinse chicken with cold water and pat dry. Rub exterior of chicken with cut surfaces of lemon. Season inside and out with salt and pepper. Place lemon halves into cavity of chicken, along with onion and herbs. Truss, if desired. Place chicken on a rack in a roasting pan. Rub butter over the outside of the chicken, or beneath the skin, between the skin and flesh, as desired. Dust with paprika. Roast 1 hour, basting once or twice as desired, until skin is crisp and juices run clear. A meat thermometer inserted into the breast should read 170C (75C), and 185F (85C) in the thigh area. Transfer chicken to a warm platter and rest 15 minutes before carving. Serve with Chicken au Jus, page 139, if desired. Makes 4 servings.

VARIATION
Fill the chicken cavity with one of the stuffings on pages 134 to 135, and omit the lemon, onion and herbs. Add an additional 20 minutes to the total roasting time. Refer to guidelines for stuffing poultry on page 133.

ROAST DUCK

A golden, crispy roast duck turns any meal into a special occasion.

1 (4-1/2- to 5-lb.) duck
Salt and freshly ground pepper to taste
1 small onion, quartered
1 small orange, quartered
Herbs of choice (optional)

TIP

After carving duck, pieces can be broiled briefly to reheat and crisp the skin.

Preheat oven to 400F (205C). Remove neck, liver, giblets and excess fat from duck and trim overhanging skin and fat from neck end; reserve for other uses. Rinse duck with cold water and pat dry. To allow fat to escape during cooking, prick duck skin all over with a fork without piercing the meat. Remove wishbone, if desired (page 18). Season inside and out with salt and pepper. Fill cavity with onion and orange or fresh herbs, if desired. Truss, if desired. Place duck breast-side up on a rack in a roasting pan. Cook in the center of the oven. Roast 1-1/4 hours, until juices run clear and a meat thermometer inserted into the thigh registers 180F (80C), removing accumulated fat from the roasting pan with a bulb baster 2 or 3 times. Transfer duck to a warm platter and rest 20 to 30 minutes before carving. Follow instructions for Chicken au Jus, page 139, to make a natural pan gravy, if desired. Makes 2 servings.

CLASSIC ROAST TURKEY

A perfect, economical meal for all year long.

1 (10- to 12-lb.) turkey
Giblet Stock (page 23) (optional)
Salt and freshly ground pepper to taste
12 tablespoons unsalted butter, melted
Stuffing of choice, or fresh herbs and
    aromatic vegetables to place in
    cavity
Giblet Gravy (page 139) (optional)

Preheat oven to 325F (165C). Remove neck and giblets from turkey and make Giblet Stock, if desired. Rinse turkey with cold water and pat dry. Season inside and out with salt and pepper. Remove wishbone, if desired (page 18). Loosely stuff neck and breast cavities with stuffing or aromatic herbs and vegetables and truss as described on page 18. Place turkey, breast-side up, on a rack in a roasting pan. Brush with a few tablespoons melted butter and immediately place in center of oven. Roast about 3 hours, basting every 20 minutes with melted butter and juices that accumulate in the pan. When turkey is done, juices should run clear yellow and a meat thermometer inserted into the bird should register 170F (75C) in the breast and 185F (85C) in the thigh. If bird has been stuffed, allow an additional 30 minutes roasting time, until stuffing reaches an internal temperature of 165F (75C). Transfer turkey to a heated platter to rest 30 minutes before carving, remove stuffing and keep warm. Make Giblet Gravy, if desired. Makes 10 to 12 servings.

Country Chicken Pot Pie

Add a bit of whimsy to this updated classic by decorating the top of the pie with a jaunty chicken cut from pastry scraps.

Savory Pie Crust (recipe below)
3 cups Chicken Stock (page 23)
3 carrots, diced
3/4 pound red potatoes, diced
2 celery stalks, diced
1/4 cup unsalted butter
1 medium-size onion, chopped
1/4 cup all-purpose flour
2-1/2 cups cubed, cooked chicken
1/2 cup fresh or frozen green peas,
   thawed if frozen
1 teaspoon chopped fresh thyme or
   1/3 teaspoon dried leaf thyme
1/8 teaspoon red (cayenne) pepper
1/2 cup minced parsley
Salt and freshly ground white pepper
   to taste
1 egg, separated
1 tablespoon cream or milk

Savory Pie Crust:

2 cups all-purpose flour
1/2 teaspoon salt
6 tablespoons unsalted butter, well
   chilled
1 large egg yolk
About 1/4 cup ice water

Make pastry and refrigerate. In a medium-size saucepan over medium-high heat, bring stock to a boil; add carrots, potatoes and celery. Reduce heat to low and simmer 7 to 10 minutes, until vegetables are barely tender. Use a slotted spoon to transfer vegetables to a large bowl, reserving the stock separately. In a small saucepan, melt butter over medium-low heat. Add onion; sauté until softened but not browned. Stir in flour and cook, stirring, until light golden-brown, about 3 minutes. Gradually whisk in 2 cups reserved warm stock and bring to a boil, whisking constantly. The remaining stock may be reserved for other use. Reduce heat to low and simmer 5 minutes. Pour sauce over reserved vegetables, gently stir in chicken, peas, thyme, cayenne and parsley; season with salt and white pepper. Cool to room temperature. If made a day in advance, cover and refrigerate filling at this point, but return to room temperature before proceeding with recipe.

Preheat oven to 425F (220C). Divide filling among 4 (2-cup) shallow baking dishes or 1 (2-quart) shallow baking dish. On a lightly floured surface, roll out pastry and cut to fit over baking dish(es) with about 1-1/2 inch overhang.

In a small bowl, lightly beat the egg white and brush some of it over the exposed surface of pastry just enough to coat and create a seal. Place pastry, egg-white-side down, over the filling. Crimp edges and brush pastry with a glaze made from the egg yolk and cream. Garnish with pastry scraps, if desired. Prick top with a fork or cut several vents to allow steam to escape while cooking. Brush once again with glaze. Bake until pastry is golden-brown, about 30 minutes. Rest 15 minutes before serving. Makes 4 servings.

Savory Pie Crust:

Combine flour and salt in a medium-size bowl. Cut in butter with a pastry blender or 2 knives until mixture resembles small peas. Mix egg yolk with 1/4 cup ice water in a small bowl and gradually add to flour, incorporating quickly with pastry blender just until mixture holds together. Add more water, if needed. Knead several times on a lightly floured surface and refrigerate, wrapped in plastic wrap, at least 1 hour. Pastry may be kept in the refrigerator up to two days, or frozen.

COUNTRY CAPTAIN

Said to have been one of President Franklin D. Roosevelt's favorites, this delectable dish is from Georgia. Serve it over plain rice and garnish with crisp bacon strips.

1 (3-lb.) chicken, cut up
1/3 cup vegetable oil
1 tablespoon bacon fat or olive oil
1 large onion, chopped
1 green bell pepper, chopped
1 large garlic clove, minced
1 cup Chicken Stock (page 23)
1 (1-lb.) can stewed tomatoes
1 teaspoon salt
1/2 teaspoon freshly ground black
   pepper
1/4 teaspoon sugar
1/2 cup raisins or currants
2 teaspoons curry powder
1 teaspoon ground thyme
1/2 cup slivered almonds, toasted

Preheat oven to 350F (175C). Rinse chicken with cold water and pat dry. In a large non-aluminum skillet, heat oil over medium-high heat. Add chicken; sauté just until browned, about 5 minutes per side. Drain chicken pieces, transfer to a casserole dish and set aside. Discard cooking oil from skillet; add bacon fat. Heat over medium heat; add onion, bell pepper and garlic. Sauté until softened but not browned. Add stock, tomatoes, salt, pepper and sugar. Bring to a boil; reduce heat and simmer 5 minutes. Stir in raisins, curry powder and thyme and pour mixture over chicken. Cover and bake 45 minutes, or until chicken is tender. Sprinkle with toasted almonds. Makes 4 servings.

QUICK & EASY

Today's cook finds poultry the ideal solution to the daily dilemma, "What's for dinner?"

There was a period not too long ago when cupboards were filled with cans and boxes of instant-this-and-that, that boasted shelf-lives of staggering longevity. Freezers overflowed with bags and pouches and little foil trays apparently designed intentionally so one frozen pea would always be diverted into the apple crisp compartment. Then came the backlash of French cuisine, when we became slaves in our own kitchens, just to be able to say, "Yes, I made it ALL from scratch!"

But rather than spending hours in the kitchen or relying on artificial or preservative-laden foods, our increasingly health-conscious population has created a demand for foods made from readily available fresh ingredients that are quick to prepare, economical and appetizing.

This chapter is devoted to recipes that are short on ingredients and preparation time, yet full of flavor and attractive in appearance. Many of these can be prepared while you watch the evening news or talk on the phone; or at the very least, prepared in a few minutes and tucked in the oven while you continue with other chores before dinner.

Save some time by keeping stock (page 23) on hand for instant sauces and soups, and compound butters (pages 136 to 137) to season grilled or roasted birds, or toss with vegetables or pasta. Pasta (page 154) is also delicious when tossed with a bit of olive oil and left over roasting juices. And whenever you're roasting a bird, consider roasting two at the same time. The second can be eaten as is, or can be used in any number of other recipes.

Orange Poached Chicken with Rosemary-Orange Pesto, page 50

Orange Poached Chicken With Rosemary-Orange Pesto

Here delicately flavored chicken is complemented by the sharp pesto flavors. Serve the chicken warm or at room temperature with bulgur and crisp-cooked green beans. Orange poached chicken breasts also make a wonderful basis for many chicken salads.

8 chicken breast halves, skinned,
    boned
Salt and freshly ground pepper to taste
1 cup fresh orange juice
11 rosemary sprigs
8 orange slices
Rosemary-Orange Pesto (page 142)

Preheat oven to 375F (190C). Rinse chicken in cold water and pat dry. Season chicken with salt and pepper; place in a single layer in a 13" x 9" baking dish. Cut a piece of parchment paper to fit snugly inside the pan; set aside. Pour orange juice over the chicken, tuck in 3 rosemary sprigs and top with parchment so it is touching the chicken. Cook 10 to 15 minutes, or until chicken is firm and opaque. Remove from oven and cool chicken in the poaching liquid. Drain and garnish with remaining rosemary and orange slices. Place a dab of pesto on top of each chicken breast and pass the remainder at the table. Makes 8 servings.

Marmalade-Baked Chicken Wings

Serve these sweet and spicy morsels as an appetizer, or with rice and steamed broccoli as an entree.

1 pound chicken wings
1 tablespoon vegetable oil
1 small shallot, coarsely chopped
1/2 cup orange marmalade or other
    marmalade
1 small gingerroot piece, peeled,
    chopped, or 1 teaspoon powdered
    ginger
1 tablespoon light soy sauce
1 teaspoon Dijon-style mustard
Juice of 1 orange (about 1/2 cup)

Preheat oven to 475F (245C). Rinse chicken in cold water and pat dry. Line a 9-inch-square pan with foil. Arrange chicken wings in a single layer in foil-lined pan. In a blender or a food processor fitted with the metal blade, process remaining ingredients together until blended. Pour mixture over chicken, coating each piece well. Cook 10 to 15 minutes, or until browned and juices run clear when chicken is pierced. Makes 2 entree servings.

Tip

To assure easy cleanup, line the inside of baking pans with foil.

CHICKEN BREASTS IN SCOTCH CREAM SAUCE

Capitalize on the elegance of this simple creation by serving each chicken breast atop a toasted crouton, garnished with a watercress sprig. Carrot puree and sautéed snow peas would make a delicious and attractive presentation.

4 Garlic Croutons (recipe below)
4 chicken breast halves, skinned, boned
1/2 cup all-purpose flour seasoned with 1 teaspoon salt, 1/2 teaspoon freshly ground white pepper and 1/2 teaspoon paprika
2 tablespoons olive oil
1/4 cup scotch whisky
3/4 cup whipping cream
Salt and freshly ground pepper
4 watercress sprigs

GARLIC CROUTONS:
4 (3/4-inch) slices cut from a loaf of good-quality French or Italian bread
2 tablespoons unsalted butter
1 tablespoon olive oil
1 garlic clove, minced

Make croutons. Rinse chicken with cold water and pat dry. Lightly dredge chicken breasts in seasoned flour. Heat olive oil in a medium-size skillet over medium heat. Add chicken; sauté until golden-brown on both sides, about 6 minutes. Transfer to a plate and keep warm. Discard fat remaining in skillet. Use whisky to deglaze the pan, scraping up any browned bits clinging to the bottom and side. Cook mixture over medium-high heat about 1 minute, and stir in the cream; then reduce heat to low and simmer about 5 minutes, until thickened. Taste seasoning, adding salt and pepper, if necessary. Place each chicken breast on a crouton and nap with cream sauce. Makes 4 servings.

Garlic Croutons:
Trim crust from each bread slice, making a neat oval pedestal for chicken breasts. Melt butter with olive oil in a medium-size skillet over low heat. Add garlic; sauté until fragrant but not browned. Increase heat to medium. Add bread; sauté until golden brown on each side, about 4 minutes. These can be made ahead and reheated 10 minutes in a 325F (165C) oven.

CHICKEN BREASTS IN TRIPLE GINGER CREAM

Ginger lovers will appreciate their favorite flavor showcased in three different forms. A combination of long grain and wild rice will complement this heavenly sauce.

8 chicken breast halves, skinned,
    boned
1/2 cup all-purpose flour
1 teaspoon ground ginger
1 teaspoon salt
1/4 teaspoon freshly ground white
    pepper
6 tablespoons unsalted butter
3 quarter-size gingerroot pieces,
    crushed with side of a knife
3 tablespoons all-purpose flour
1 cup Chicken Stock (page 23)
1 cup half and half
4 tablespoons minced crystallized
    ginger

Rinse chicken with cold water and pat dry. Place chicken breasts between two sheets of waxed paper and pound until 1/4 inch thick. Combine flour, ground ginger, salt and pepper in a paper bag and add breasts one or two at a time, shaking first to coat well, then to shake off any excess. Melt butter in a large skillet over medium heat. Add gingerroot; sauté until fragrant. Add chicken; sauté until golden, about 3 minutes per side. Remove breasts to a platter and keep warm. Discard gingerroot, but save the cooking juices. Over low heat, add flour to the remaining juices in the pan and stir about 3 minutes. Whisk in stock and half and half; cook, whisking until smooth and thickened. Stir in 2 tablespoons of the crystallized ginger and taste sauce to adjust seasonings, adding more salt, pepper and ground ginger, if necessary. Serve sauce over chicken. Garnish with remaining 2 tablespoons crystallized ginger. Makes 8 servings.

BLUE MONDAY CHICKEN

For economy sake, you may want to substitute other chicken parts for boneless breasts, adding an extra 15 minutes or so to the baking time. Serve this with rice cooked in chicken broth (page 150) and a crisp spinach salad.

8 chicken breast halves, skinned,
    boned
Salt and freshly ground white pepper
    to taste
1/4 cup unsalted butter
2 cups (1 pint) dairy sour cream
8 ounces blue cheese, crumbled
2 large garlic cloves, minced
1 tablespoon brandy (optional)
1/4 cup sliced almonds

Preheat oven to 350F (175C). Rinse chicken with cold water and pat dry. Season chicken with salt and pepper. Melt butter in a large skillet over medium-high heat. Add chicken; sauté only until both sides are lightly browned, about 6 minutes. Butter a shallow 2-quart baking dish; arrange chicken breasts in a single layer in dish. In a medium-size bowl, mix sour cream, cheese, garlic and brandy, if desired; pour over the chicken. Sprinkle almonds on top. Bake 30 minutes, until hot and bubbly and chicken is cooked through. Makes 8 servings.

TURKEY IN THE STRAW

The Italian dish "Hay and Straw" combines thin strands of green and yellow pasta. Here I've taken inspiration from a favorite childhood song to update this tasty and colorful classic.

8 ounces Spinach Pasta (page 154), cut into thin strands about 1/8 to 1/10 inch wide
8 ounces Basic Pasta (page 154), cut into same width as Spinach Pasta
6 ounces cooked turkey meat, chopped
1/2 cup unsalted butter
Salt and freshly ground pepper to taste
3/4 cup half and half
1/2 cup freshly grated Parmesan cheese

Cook pastas as directed. Melt 1/4 cup of the butter in a large skillet over medium heat. Add turkey; sauté until hot. Season with salt and pepper. Reduce heat to low; add half and half and cook, stirring, until slightly thickened. Drain pasta and toss in a large bowl with the remaining butter. Add turkey in cream sauce and half of the cheese, tossing again. Serve immediately, offering remaining cheese separately. Makes 4 to 6 servings.

TURKEY CUTLETS WITH CRANBERRY CHUTNEY

These quick and crispy cutlets go well with Make-Ahead Mashed Potatoes (page 148). Serve with lemon wedges to enhance the flavor of the turkey.

8 turkey cutlets (about 1-1/2 lbs.)
1/4 cup all-purpose flour, seasoned with salt and freshly ground pepper
1 egg, lightly beaten
1/2 cup fresh or dried bread crumbs
1/4 cup unsalted butter
1/4 cup olive oil
Cranberry Chutney (page 144)

Rinse turkey with cold water and pat dry. Dredge cutlets lightly in seasoned flour. Dip both sides in egg and then in bread crumbs. Place on a rack to dry 10 to 15 minutes. In a large skillet, melt butter with olive oil over medium-high heat. Add breaded cutlets; sauté until brown and crusty, about 1 to 2 minutes per side. Serve immediately with Cranberry Chutney. Makes 8 servings.

TURKEY PICCATA

Buying already cut turkey cutlets at the market makes this dish a snap. Fresh steamed broccoli and orzo (rice-shaped pasta) tossed with butter and Parmesan cheese completes the meal.

6 turkey cutlets (about 1-1/4 lbs.)
1/2 cup all-purpose flour
2 teaspoons salt
1/4 teaspoon freshly ground pepper
Dash of red (cayenne) pepper
1/4 cup unsalted butter
1 tablespoon olive oil
2 tablespoons dry white wine or
    vermouth
3 tablespoons fresh lemon juice
3 tablespoons capers, drained
1/4 cup minced parsley
1 lemon, very thinly sliced, for
    garnish

Rinse turkey with cold water and pat dry. Place turkey cutlets between 2 sheets of waxed paper and pound until 1/4 inch thick. Season flour with salt, pepper and cayenne; lightly dredge the turkey pieces in seasoned flour, shaking off excess flour. Melt butter with olive oil in a large skillet over medium heat. Add turkey cutlets, a few at a time; sauté 1 or 2 minutes on each side. Remove from heat, drain on paper towels and keep warm. Discard all but 2 tablespoons of cooking fat. Over medium-high heat, stir wine into skillet, loosening the browned bits that cling to the bottom and side. Stir in the lemon juice; reduce heat to low. Return turkey pieces to pan to coat with the sauce. Garnish with a sprinkling of capers and parsley and lemon slices. Makes 6 servings.

CHICKEN WITH HOT TOMATO VINAIGRETTE

I've chosen the cool, fresh flavor of mint to enhance this light and lively sauce. This is delicious with a Greek-style salad made with torn romaine lettuce, olives, cucumber, green onions and feta cheese. Crusty bread is a must for savoring the last drop of sauce.

1 to 1-1/2 quarts Chicken Stock (page
    23)
6 chicken breast halves, boned

HOT TOMATO VINAIGRETTE:
1/2 cup olive oil
1 large garlic clove, minced
4 large tomatoes, peeled, seeded and
    diced
1 teaspoon sugar
1 tablespoon balsamic vinegar or
    lemon juice
Salt and freshly ground pepper
2 tablespoons finely chopped mint
    leaves

Bring Chicken Stock to a simmer in a 5-quart pot with a cover. Rinse chicken with cold water and pat dry. Place chicken breasts in a single layer; simmer, covered, 20 minutes, or just until cooked through. Remove from heat and keep in warm stock while making vinaigrette. Make vinaigrette. To serve, remove chicken from stock; reserve stock for other use, if desired. Remove skin from chicken; place each piece on a plate. Spoon about 2 tablespoons of hot vinaigrette over the top of each serving. Makes 6 servings.

HOT TOMATO VINAIGRETTE:
Heat olive oil in a large skillet over medium-low heat. Add garlic and sauté until fragrant but not browned. Add tomatoes and sugar; sauté about 2 minutes, until heated through. Add vinegar, salt, pepper and mint and adjust seasonings to taste.

Turkey Piccata

JUST DUCKY MOSTACCIOLI

The preparation of this delicacy was inspired by Biba Caggiano's "Pennette 3 Vasselle." The uncooked pasta is sautéed in olive oil and then cooked in a manner similar to risotto, resulting in a very rich and creamy dish. All that is needed to round out the meal is a tossed green salad in a light vinaigrette. This is an excellent use for leftover duck or Confit (page 30), or buy cooked duck from a deli or Chinese restaurant.

5 tablespoons olive oil

1 small onion, thinly sliced

2 medium-size carrots, diced

8 ounces fresh mushrooms, preferably a mixture of wild and cultivated, thinly sliced

1 large garlic clove, finely chopped

3 tablespoons chopped parsley, preferably flat-leaf Italian

2 teaspoons chopped thyme leaves or 1/2 teaspoon dried leaf thyme

2 teaspoons balsamic vinegar

Salt and freshly ground black pepper to taste

8 ounces mostaccioli, pennette or other tubular pasta

2 tablespoons armagnac or brandy

1-1/4 cups Duck Stock (page 23), or Chicken Stock (page 23)

1/2 cup whipping cream

2 teaspoons whole green peppercorns in vinegar, drained

1/2 (4-1/2- to 5-lb.) duck, cooked (page 45), with skin and bones discarded or reserved for other uses (about 1 pound of meat)

3 tablespoons freshly grated Parmesan cheese

Heat 3 tablespoons of the olive oil in a large skillet over medium-high heat. Add onion, carrots and mushrooms; sauté until softened but not browned. Stir in garlic, parsley and thyme; cook until liquid evaporates. Add vinegar; cook until evaporated. Season with salt and pepper. Remove vegetable mixture with a spoon; set aside. Heat remaining 2 tablespoons olive oil in the same large skillet over medium heat. Add pasta; sauté until golden-brown. Add armagnac and stir until evaporated. Stir in 1/2 cup of the stock; cook over medium heat until pasta absorbs the stock. Add another 1/2 cup stock and the cream; cook until stock evaporates. Return the sautéed vegetables to the pan along with peppercorns and duck. Add remaining 1/4 cup stock; cook a few minutes longer, until pasta is tender and sauce is thick. Stir in cheese and serve immediately. Makes 6 first-course servings or 4 entree servings.

Chicken In Garlic Butter

Don't be intimidated by the amount of garlic; its flavor mellows in the cooking. This very simple, garlic-lovers treat goes beautifully with steamed, tiny new potatoes and a baked tomato half.

6 chicken breast halves, skinned,
    boned
1/2 cup unsalted butter
12 whole garlic cloves, peeled
1 garlic clove, finely minced
1 bunch Italian parsley, finely
    chopped
Juice of 1 lemon (2 tablespoons)
Salt and freshly ground white pepper
    to taste

Rinse chicken in cold water and pat dry. In a large skillet over low heat, melt butter. Add whole and minced garlic cloves. Sauté until whole cloves are tender but not browned, about 10 minutes. Increase heat to medium-high; add chicken. Sauté until lightly browned. Reduce heat to medium and simmer until chicken is cooked through, about 10 minutes. Remove chicken to a warm platter. Stir parsley and lemon juice into garlic butter in the skillet; adjust seasonings, if necessary, and pour over chicken. When serving, give each person 2 whole cooked garlic cloves. Makes 6 servings.

Chicken In Creamy Mustard Sauce

This piquant sauce is a perfect foil for chicken breasts, but it works equally well with other chicken parts.

3 tablespoons unsalted butter
2 tablespoons olive oil or vegetable oil
6 chicken breast halves, skinned,
    boned
Salt and freshly ground white pepper
    to taste
3 shallots, finely chopped
1/4 cup dry white wine, brandy or
    Chicken Stock (page 23)
1 cup (1/2 pint) whipping cream
1/4 cup Dijon-style mustard

Rinse chicken in cold water and pat dry. Melt 2 tablespoons of the butter with the olive oil in a large skillet over medium heat. Season chicken breasts with salt and pepper. Add chicken to skillet; sauté until just cooked through and browned, about 6 minutes. Remove chicken and set aside on a warm platter. Discard cooking fat; add the remaining 1 tablespoon of butter to the same skillet over medium heat. Add shallots; sauté until tender but not browned. Deglaze skillet with the wine, loosening any browned bits clinging to the bottom and side of the skillet. Increase heat to medium-high and whisk in the cream and mustard; blend well. Cook, stirring until the sauce has reduced and thickened, about 5 minutes. Spoon sauce over chicken breasts and serve immediately. Makes 6 servings.

CHICKEN IN MADEIRA CREAM

The luscious flavor of this dish belies its simple preparation.

4 chicken breast halves, boned,
    skinned
5 tablespoons unsalted butter
8 ounces fresh mushrooms, sliced
1 tablespoon chopped parsley
Salt and freshly ground white pepper
Paprika
1 cup (1/2 pint) whipping cream
1/4 cup Madeira or sherry

Rinse chicken breasts in cold water and pat dry. Melt 2 tablespoons of the butter in a large skillet over medium heat. Add mushrooms and parsley; sauté until golden, about 5 minutes. Remove mushrooms; set aside. Season chicken breasts with salt, pepper and paprika. Melt 2 tablespoons of the butter in same skillet over medium heat. Add chicken; sauté until lightly browned, about 6 minutes. Remove from pan and set aside. Melt the remaining 1 tablespoon butter in the skillet; stir in the cream and Madeira until well blended. Return chicken and mushrooms to the skillet and simmer, uncovered, until tender, about 5 minutes. Makes 4 servings.

CHICKEN THIGHS BALSAMICO

Balsamic vinegar comes from Modena, Italy, where it is aged in wooden casks for at least 10 years. It is highly aromatic, with a haunting sweet/tart flavor. It is often used sparingly, or in tandem with other vinegars, but in this recipe its unique flavor takes center stage. (Don't bother serving an expensive wine, as the vinegar will overpower it.) Plain fusilli, boiled and tossed with olive oil and Parmesan cheese, makes a nice accompaniment.

6 chicken thighs
2 tablespoons dried currants
1/2 cup boiling water
Kosher salt and coarsely ground
    pepper to taste
1 tablespoon Garlic Oil (page 21)
1/4 cup balsamic vinegar
1 tablespoon Dijon-style mustard
1/2 cup Chicken Stock (page 23)
Zest of 1 orange or lemon, finely
    chopped
1 tablespoon chopped fresh marjoram
    leaves or 1 teaspoon dried leaf
    marjoram
1/4 teaspoon sugar (optional)
Marjoram leaves and orange slices, for
    garnish

Rinse chicken in cold water and pat dry. Place currants in a small bowl and cover with boiling water. Set aside. Season chicken with salt and pepper. Heat Garlic Oil in a large skillet over medium-high heat. Add chicken, skin-side down; sauté 5 minutes, or until crispy brown. Reduce heat to medium-low, turn the chicken pieces over and cook 12 to 15 minutes, or until cooked through. Remove chicken from pan, drain on paper towels and place on a serving platter.

Discard cooking fat in skillet; return skillet to medium-high heat and deglaze with vinegar, scraping up any bits of chicken clinging to the bottom and side of skillet. Whisk in mustard until completely blended. As the vinegar continues to reduce over the heat, whisk in stock and cook until slightly syrupy, about 2 minutes. Drain currants, discarding water, and add to sauce with the orange zest and marjoram. Remove from heat and season with salt and pepper, if necessary. If the sauce is too acidic, stir sugar into the hot sauce to neutralize the acid. Spoon the sauce over chicken and serve hot or at room temperature. Garnish with marjoram leaves and orange slices. Makes 3 servings.

Oven-fried Chicken Italiano

There's no need to bake your chicken in pricey packaged products from the supermarket. Serve with buttered noodles tossed with Parmesan cheese and steamed zucchini, napped in tomato sauce.

1 (3-1/2-lb.) chicken, cut into 8
    pieces
1/2 cup unsalted butter, melted
1 garlic clove, finely minced
1-1/2 cups dry bread crumbs
1 teaspoon salt
Freshly ground pepper to taste
2 tablespoons finely chopped parsley
1 tablespoon finely chopped fresh
    oregano leaves, or 1 teaspoon dried
    leaf oregano
2 teaspoons finely chopped fresh
    rosemary leaves, or 1/2 teaspoon
    dried rosemary
1/4 teaspoon red (cayenne) pepper

Preheat oven to 350F (175C). Lightly grease a 13" x 9" baking dish. Rinse chicken in cold water and pat dry. Combine melted butter with garlic in a shallow dish. Dip chicken pieces to coat completely. Combine bread crumbs and seasonings in a paper bag. Add chicken pieces, 1 or 2 at a time, and shake until well coated. Place chicken pieces skin-side up in greased dish; bake 45 minutes, or until juices run clear when chicken is pierced with a fork. Makes 6 servings.

Variation
Substitute 1/2 cup grated Parmesan cheese for 1/2 cup of the bread crumbs.

Chicken Thighs With Sherry & Fresh Mushrooms

Serve this comforting dish over buttered egg noodles for a satisfying winter meal. Fresh steamed broccoli makes a colorful addition to the dinner plate.

6 chicken thighs
1/4 cup all-purpose flour
1/2 teaspoon freshly grated nutmeg
2 teaspoons salt
Freshly ground pepper to taste
1/4 cup unsalted butter
1 cup Chicken Stock (page 23)
1/2 cup dry sherry or other wine
8 ounces fresh mushrooms, halved if
    large
1/4 cup minced onion
1 tablespoon finely chopped parsley

Rinse chicken in cold water and pat dry. Mix flour, nutmeg, salt and pepper together in a paper bag. Add chicken thighs, 1 or 2 at a time; shake until well coated. Melt butter in a large skillet or dutch oven over medium-high heat. Add chicken; brown both sides of the thighs, turning, about 5 minutes. Add stock, sherry, mushrooms and onion. Reduce heat, cover and simmer until meat is tender, 20 minutes. Sprinkle with parsley. Makes 3 servings.

Pasta With Turkey, Chard & Parmesan Cream Sauce

Any pasta will do for this dish, but I love Bell Pepper Pasta (page 155) made with red bell pepper.

Parmesan Cream Sauce (recipe below)
3 to 5 tablespoons olive oil
1/3 cup pine nuts
2 large garlic cloves, minced
1 large bunch Swiss chard, coarsely
  chopped
2 cups cubed, cooked turkey breast
  meat
1 pound Bell Pepper Pasta (page 155),
  cut into 1/4-inch-wide strips
Salt and freshly ground pepper to taste

PARMESAN CREAM SAUCE:
3 tablespoons unsalted butter
1 shallot, minced
3 tablespoons all-purpose flour
2-1/2 cups milk
1/2 cup whipping cream
1/8 teaspoon freshly grated nutmeg
1 cup (3 oz.) freshly grated Parmesan
  cheese
Salt and freshly ground white pepper
  to taste

Make sauce. Warm 3 tablespoons olive oil in a large skillet over low heat. Add pine nuts; sauté until lightly browned. Remove with a slotted spoon and set aside. Increase heat to medium-high. Add garlic and chard; sauté until just softened, about 1 minute. Toss in turkey and stir-fry just until warm, adding more olive oil, if necessary. Cook and drain the pasta as directed and toss with nuts, turkey mixture and cream sauce. Taste for seasoning. Serve immediately. Makes 4 to 6 servings.

PARMESAN CREAM SAUCE:
Melt butter in a medium-size saucepan over low heat. Add shallot; sauté until softened but not browned. Stir in flour; cook, stirring, 3 or 4 minutes. Meanwhile, in a separate pan, heat milk and cream until almost boiling, then gradually whisk into the flour mixture. Return to low heat and simmer 15 to 20 minutes, stirring frequently. Season with nutmeg and remove from heat. Stir in Parmesan cheese and season with salt and pepper, if necessary.

Southwestern Turkey Wings

These wings are equally delicious cold so you may want to make extras for tomorrow's lunch.

4 pounds turkey wings
6 tablespoons unsalted butter, melted
1 teaspoon lime juice or lemon juice
2 teaspoons chili powder
1 teaspoon ground cumin
1 garlic clove, crushed
1 teaspoon salt
Dash of red (cayenne) pepper

Preheat oven to 350F (175C). Lightly oil a baking dish large enough to hold wings in 1 layer. Rinse turkey with cold water and pat dry. Arrange wings in a single layer in oiled baking dish. In a small bowl, combine butter, lime juice, chili powder, cumin, garlic, salt and cayenne. Generously brush both sides of wings with the butter mixture; bake 30 minutes. Turn and baste again with butter mixture. Reduce oven temperature to 325F (165C) and bake 30 minutes more or until tender when pierced with a fork. Makes 4 servings.

Pasta with Turkey, Chard & Parmesan Cream Sauce

CHICKEN LIVERS WITH APPLES & ONIONS

Here's a new twist on liver and onions. Begin by cooking a pot of rice (page 150) for an accompaniment. By the time the rice is done, your entree will be ready to serve, too.

1 tablespoon olive or vegetable oil
3 bacon slices, cut into 1/2-inch pieces
1/4 cup all-purpose flour
1/2 teaspoon salt
1/4 teaspoon freshly ground pepper
1-1/2 pounds chicken livers
1 medium-size onion, thinly sliced
2 medium-size tart apples, pared, cored
    and thinly sliced
1/4 cup Calvados, brandy or Chicken
    Stock (page 23)
1 tablespoon unsalted butter (optional)
1 tablespoon chopped parsley

Heat oil in a large skillet over medium heat. Add bacon; sauté until barely cooked, about 3 minutes. Mix flour, salt and pepper together in a paper bag. Carefully trim, rinse and drain the livers, discarding any portions tinged with green. Add chicken livers to the flour mixture; shake until coated. Add chicken livers, onion and apples to the bacon and cook until onion is tender and lightly browned. Using a slotted spoon, remove livers, onion, bacon and apples to a serving platter and discard fat from skillet. Return pan to medium-high heat and deglaze with calvados, scraping up any bits that cling to the bottom and side of the skillet. Whisk in butter, if desired, and pour sauce over chicken livers. Garnish with chopped parsley. Makes 6 servings.

TURKEY CUTLETS IN LEMON CREAM SAUCE

This rich sauce is equally delicious over poached chicken breasts.

8 turkey cutlets (about 1-1/2 lbs.)
Salt and freshly ground white pepper
    to taste
Juice of 1 lemon
4 tablespoons unsalted butter
Juice of 3 lemons
1 cup Chicken Stock (page 23)
4 egg yolks
Zest of 1/2 lemon
3 tablespoons chopped parsley, for
    garnish

Rinse turkey in cold water and pat dry. Season turkey with salt, pepper and juice of 1 lemon; set aside. Melt 2 tablespoons of the butter in a large skillet over medium-high heat. Add turkey; sauté on both sides until cooked through, about 4 minutes. Remove to a warm platter and set aside. In a heavy 1-1/2-quart saucepan, heat remaining 2 tablespoons butter with remaining lemon juice and the stock until it barely reaches a boil. Remove from heat and set aside. Meanwhile, whisk egg yolks in a small bowl. Very gradually, whisk in 1/3 cup of the hot liquid, then whisk yolk mixture into the remaining liquid. Add zest and whisk over very low heat until thickened. (Excessive heat will curdle the yolks). Spoon sauce over turkey and garnish with parsley. Makes 8 servings.

Chicken Drumsticks In Orange & Almond Sauce

Serve this sweet and spicy delight with rice pilaf, garnished with orange twists.

12 chicken drumsticks
2 tablespoons olive oil or vegetable oil
Salt and freshly ground pepper to taste
1 teaspoon ground ginger
2 tablespoons unsalted butter
Juice of 2 oranges (about 1 cup)
Zest of 1 orange, finely chopped
1 tablespoon Dijon-style mustard
1/3 cup sliced almonds, toasted

Rinse chicken in cold water and pat dry. Heat olive oil in a large skillet over medium heat. Add chicken drumsticks; cook 5 to 7 minutes. Season with salt, pepper and ginger. Remove chicken, set aside and discard oil. To the same skillet, add butter, scraping up any bits of chicken clinging to the bottom and side of the skillet. Add orange juice, zest, mustard and chicken; cook until chicken is tender, about 15 minutes. Arrange chicken on a platter. Spoon sauce over chicken; top with toasted almonds. Makes 6 servings.

Chicken Oreganato

This is a very simple dish with Greek overtones. Reserve a few oregano sprigs to garnish the serving platter.

1 (3-1/2-lb.) chicken, cut up
1/3 cup chopped fresh oregano leaves
   or 2 tablespoons dried leaf oregano
1/4 cup olive oil
Salt and freshly ground pepper to taste
1 teaspoon paprika
Juice of 1 lemon (2 tablespoons)

Preheat oven to 450F (230C). Rinse chicken in cold water and pat dry. Lightly oil a 13" x 9" shallow baking pan and set aside. In a small bowl, mix all ingredients (except chicken) together. Rub mixture into both sides of each chicken piece and place in the prepared pan. Bake 45 minutes, or until juices run clear when chicken is pierced with a fork. Makes 6 servings.

Brandied Chicken Thighs L'Orange

I love this with Onion & Rice Soubise (page 151) and steamed fresh asparagus.

12 chicken thighs
Salt and freshly ground white pepper
3 tablespoons Garlic Oil (page 21) or
    other olive oil
1 (6-oz.) can frozen orange juice
    concentrate
1/4 cup brandy
1 tablespoon unsalted butter
1 tablespoon chopped fresh tarragon
    leaves, or 1 teaspoon dried leaf
    tarragon

Preheat oven to 375F (190C). Lightly butter a 13" x 9" baking dish; set aside. Rinse chicken in cold water and pat dry. Season chicken pieces with salt and pepper. Heat oil in a large skillet over medium-high heat. Add chicken thighs, in batches, if necessary; sauté until browned, turning, about 10 minutes. Meanwhile, in a small saucepan, heat the orange juice concentrate and brandy with the remaining ingredients just until combined. Remove chicken from skillet and drain on paper towels. Place chicken thighs in a single layer in the prepared pan and pour orange mixture over them. Bake about 15 minutes or until chicken is thoroughly cooked. Makes 6 servings.

Warm Chicken Liver Salad With Pistachios

Economical and easy, serve this warm salad as an entree.

3 cups curly endive leaves
8 ounces chicken livers
1/4 cup olive oil (or a combination of
    olive oil and walnut oil)
2 tablespoons chopped toasted
    pistachios
2 tablespoons wine vinegar or lemon
    juice
Salt and freshly ground pepper to taste

Arrange the endive on 2 salad plates and set aside. Carefully trim, rinse and drain the livers, discarding any portions tinged with green. Coarsely chop livers into large chunks, if desired. Heat oil in a wok or large skillet over medium-high heat. Add livers; sauté until barely cooked, 2 or 3 minutes. Quickly stir in the pistachios, vinegar, salt and pepper. Divide the mixture, including the cooking liquid, equally between the two salads. Serve immediately. Makes 2 servings.

CHICKEN BREASTS WITH LEMON-CAPER BUTTER

This piquant sauce is thickened by a mixture of butter and flour called beurre manié. *You can keep a batch of this mixture on hand in your freezer.*

6 chicken breast halves, skinned, boned
1/4 cup plus 2 teaspoons unsalted butter
2 tablespoons fresh lemon juice
Zest of 1 lemon, finely chopped
2 tablespoons vermouth or dry white wine
2 tablespoon capers, drained
2 garlic cloves, minced
2 teaspoons all-purpose flour
Salt and freshly ground white pepper to taste
2 tablespoons chopped fresh parsley

Rinse chicken in cold water and pat dry. In a large skillet over medium heat, melt the 1/4 cup butter. Add lemon juice, zest, wine, capers and garlic; cook until bubbling. Add chicken; reduce heat to low, cover and simmer 20 minutes. Uncover and simmer 10 minutes more. Remove chicken and place on a warm platter. Meanwhile, mix the 2 teaspoons butter and the flour in a small bowl until thoroughly combined. Gradually whisk bits of butter mixture into cooking juices in pan to thicken. Season with salt and pepper. Pour sauce over chicken, sprinkle with parsley and serve immediately. Makes 6 servings.

DILLY BAKED CHICKEN BREASTS

Enjoy garden-fresh flavor in only a few minutes. Try this with steamed carrots and new potatoes.

4 chicken breast halves, skinned, boned
1/2 cup Basic Mayonnaise (page 141) or commercial mayonnaise
1/2 cup dairy sour cream
1 small garlic clove, minced
2 teaspoons fresh lemon juice
3 tablespoons chopped fresh dill weed or 1 tablespoon dried dill weed
Salt and freshly ground pepper to taste

Preheat oven to 450F (230C). Grease a baking dish large enough to hold chicken in 1 layer. Rinse chicken breasts in cold water and pat dry. Arrange chicken in a single layer in greased baking dish. In a small bowl, mix mayonnaise, sour cream, garlic, lemon juice and dill. Season with salt and pepper. Spread sauce over chicken breasts. Bake 12 to 15 minutes or until cooked through. Makes 4 servings.

GAME HENS WITH MAPLE-PEAR SAUCE

For a real timesaver, canned pears packed in their own juice will work surprisingly well for this sauce.

2 Cornish game hens, split in half
Salt and freshly ground black pepper
   to taste
1/4 cup unsalted butter
1 tablespoon olive oil

MAPLE-PEAR SAUCE:
1/2 cup maple syrup
Chopped leaves from 2 thyme sprigs
   or 1-1/2 teaspoons dried leaf thyme
1/2 cup Chicken Stock (page 23)
1 tablespoon fresh lemon juice
2 cups coarsely chopped, peeled ripe
   pears
1 cup (1/2 pint) whipping cream
8 tablespoons unsalted butter, softened
Salt and freshly ground white pepper
   to taste

Rinse hens with cold water and pat dry. Season inside and out with salt and pepper. In a large skillet over medium-high heat, melt butter with oil. Add hens and sauté until browned on all sides. Reduce heat to low, cover and cook until hens are tender, about 20 minutes. Meanwhile, make sauce. Drizzle a bit of sauce over each game hen half. Makes 2 to 4 servings.

MAPLE-PEAR SAUCE:
In a medium-size non-aluminum saucepan over medium-low heat, gently warm the maple syrup and thyme. Stir in stock, lemon juice and pears and increase heat to medium, cooking until mixture is reduced by half. Stir in cream and boil until slightly thickened. Reduce heat, whisk in butter a tablespoon at a time and cook, stirring, until sauce is smooth. Season with salt and pepper.

HONEY-PECAN DRUMSTICKS

The bread crumbs and pecans add an interesting nutty flavor and crunch.

16 chicken drumsticks
2 tablespoons unsalted butter
1/4 cup honey
2 tablespoons Dijon-style mustard
1/4 teaspoon red (cayenne) pepper
1/2 teaspoon salt
1/2 cup fresh bread crumbs
1/2 cup finely chopped pecans

Preheat oven to 350F (175C). Rinse chicken in cold water and pat dry. Line a 13" x 9" baking pan with foil; arrange drumsticks in foil-lined pan. In a small saucepan over medium-low heat, melt butter, then stir in the honey, mustard, salt and cayenne. Simmer until well combined, about 2 minutes. Remove from heat. Using a pastry brush, brush chicken generously with all of the honey mixture. In a small bowl, combine bread crumbs and pecans and sprinkle over chicken. Bake 50 to 60 minutes until juices run clear when pierced. (If chicken browns too quickly, cover the pan loosely with foil.) Serve warm. Makes 6 to 8 servings.

JOYCE'S CHICKEN WITH PINEAPPLE

This recipe comes from my colleague Joyce Jue, an internationally recognized authority on Asian cuisine. Add only steamed rice for a wonderful meal.

1 Crispy Roast Chicken (page **44**),
   meat and skin removed from bones
1/4 cup Chicken Stock (page **23**)
1 to 2 teaspoons minced gingerroot
2 tablespoons brown sugar
2 tablespoons red wine vinegar
1 tablespoon dark soy sauce
1 tablespoon peanut oil or corn oil
1/2 teaspoon kosher salt
1 onion, cut into 1-inch pieces
1 red bell pepper, cut into 1-inch
   pieces
1 cup cubed fresh pineapple (1-inch
   cubes)

Cut the boned chicken meat and skin into 2" x 3/4" strips and set aside. In a small bowl, mix the stock, gingerroot, brown sugar, vinegar and soy sauce; set aside. Over high heat, preheat wok until hot. Add oil and salt, swirling to coat side of wok. When oil is hot, add onion and bell pepper; stir-fry until peppers are bright red, about 1 minute. Add stock mixture and toss together over high heat until well mixed. Toss in reserved chicken and stir-fry quickly until heated through, about 15 seconds. Toss in pineapple and stir-fry 10 seconds more. Serve immediately. Makes 4 servings.

SPICY CHICKEN & WALNUTS

Serve this with rice and Chinese yard-long beans.

4 chicken breast halves, skinned,
   boned
1 egg
1 teaspoon cornstarch
1 tablespoon Chicken Stock (page
   23), or water
1 tablespoon bourbon or dry sherry
1/2 teaspoon sugar
3 tablespoons soy sauce
3 tablespoons peanut oil
8 green onions, cut on the diagonal
   into 2-inch lengths
2 garlic cloves, minced
2 thin gingerroot slices, peeled,
   minced
1/2 to 1 teaspoon dried red pepper
   flakes
1 cup walnut halves

Rinse chicken in cold water and pat dry. Cut chicken into bite-size cubes. In a medium-size bowl, mix together the egg, cornstarch, stock, bourbon, sugar, soy sauce and chicken; set aside. Heat a wok or large heavy skillet over medium-high heat; add 2 tablespoons of the oil, swirling to cover the surface. Add chicken; stir-fry 3 to 5 minutes, until opaque. Remove from wok; add the remaining tablespoon of oil to wok. Add onions, garlic and gingerroot; stir-fry about 1 minute. Add reserved bourbon mixture, chicken, pepper flakes and walnuts; stir-fry until heated through, 1 or 2 minutes. Serve immediately. Makes 4 servings.

OIL SHOWERED CHICKEN

Allowing time for the chicken to rest after steaming is an important step in this recipe.

4 green onions
1 teaspoon gingerroot, minced
1 tablespoon salt
1 tablespoon medium-dry sherry
1 (3-lb.) chicken
1/4 cup peanut oil
1/2 cup fresh orange juice
1/2 teaspoon sugar
1 teaspoon soy sauce
2 teaspoons cornstarch mixed with 1
   tablespoon water

Mince 1 green onion and combine in a small bowl with gingerroot, salt and sherry. Rinse chicken with cold water, pat dry, then rub with salt mixture. Cover loosely and set aside. Place chicken, breast-side up, in a heatproof bowl placed on a steamer rack over high heat. Steam over vigorously boiling water 25 minutes. Remove bowl of chicken and rest 20 minutes. Drain cooking liquid from chicken. While chicken is cooling, in a saucepan or wok, combine orange juice, sugar, soy sauce and 1/2 cup liquid from chicken. Bring to a boil, thicken with cornstarch mixture and keep warm over low heat. Chop chicken Chinese style (see below). Finely shred remaining green onions into 3-inch strips and spread over top of chicken. Heat peanut oil just until it begins to smoke. Be sure to watch it carefully. Drizzle smoking oil over chicken, then the orange sauce. Serve immediately. Makes 4 servings.

Note: To chop chicken Chinese style: With a heavy cleaver, cut through back and breast to halve chicken; remove thighs and drumsticks at first joint; remove wings, cleave each half of chicken body the long way, then into inch-wide pieces. Use the cleaver to lift each half to serving platter, retaining original chicken shape; chop the thigh, drumsticks and wings (retaining shape), and place them also in original position.

SWEET & SOUR CHICKEN

Nothing could be simpler than this tried and true favorite.

1 (3-lb.) chicken, cut into serving
   pieces
1 small onion, chopped
1/4 cup chopped green bell pepper
1 (15-oz.) can tomato sauce
1 tablespoon soy sauce
1/3 cup cider vinegar
2-1/2 cups coarsely chopped fresh
   pineapple, including juice
1/4 cup packed brown sugar
1 teaspoon dry mustard
Salt and freshly ground black pepper
   to taste

Preheat oven to 375F (190C). Rinse chicken pieces with cold water and pat dry. Place in a single layer in a non-aluminum baking dish. In a medium-size bowl, combine the onion, bell pepper, tomato sauce, soy sauce, vinegar, pineapple, brown sugar, mustard, salt and black pepper. Pour over chicken and bake, covered, 30 minutes. Uncover and bake an additional 15 minutes or until chicken is tender. Makes 4 servings.

STIR-FRIED CITRUS CHICKEN

Try this same luscious sauce with chicken wings or drumsticks. And don't forget the steamed rice!

Marinade (recipe below)
2 chicken breast halves, skinned, boned
2 teaspoons vegetable oil
1/4 cup Chicken Stock (page 23)
2 tablespoons fresh lemon juice
1/4 cup fresh orange juice
1-1/2 tablespoons brown sugar
1 tablespoon dry white wine or vermouth
4 thin lemon slices
2 thin orange slices
2 teaspoons cornstarch mixed with 1 tablespoon water
Additional lemon or orange slices for garnish

MARINADE:
1 teaspoon minced gingerroot
2 teaspoons dry white wine or vermouth
1/2 teaspoon salt
Dash of freshly ground pepper

Make marinade. Rinse chicken with cold water and pat dry. Cut chicken breast into 1-1/2-inch-square pieces. Add to Marinade and marinate 30 minutes. Heat oil in wok or skillet over high heat; stir-fry chicken 1-1/2 to 2 minutes. Add stock, lemon and orange juices, sugar and wine; mix well. Reduce heat to low, cover and simmer 2 minutes. Add lemon and orange slices and simmer 1 minute. Thicken with cornstarch mixture, mixing in well. Spoon into a bowl and garnish with citrus slices. Serves 3 or 4 with other dishes.

DEVILED DRUMSTICKS

These quick and spicy chicken drumsticks are great for picnics.

20 to 24 chicken drumsticks
1/3 cup olive oil
1/2 cup Dijon-style mustard
1/3 cup dry white wine
1 teaspoon salt
1/2 teaspoon red (cayenne) pepper
Freshly ground black pepper to taste
1/4 cup finely chopped shallots
1-1/2 cups fresh bread crumbs

Preheat oven to 350F (175C). Rinse drumsticks in cold water and pat dry. Line a 17" x 11" baking pan with foil. Using a pastry brush, coat all sides of chicken with oil and arrange on the foil-lined pan. In a small bowl, mix together the mustard, wine, salt, cayenne, black pepper and shallots; generously brush this mixture over the chicken. Sprinkle bread crumbs over top. Bake 50 to 60 minutes or until juices run clear when chicken is pierced. (If chicken browns too quickly, cover the pan loosely with foil.) Serve warm or at room temperature. Makes 8 to 10 servings.

LIGHT MEALS

*L*ight meals does not necessarily mean dinners for calorie counters, though many of these recipes fit into that category. And light never refers to a lack of taste or satisfaction, since these zesty dishes highlight contrasts in texture and flavor. In this chapter you'll find an assortment of uncomplicated, new-fashioned ideas designed to fill the demand for straightforward and refreshing one-dish meals—a far cry from the over-sauced, overbaked and overwrought casseroles of the not-too-distant past.

Versatility is the key ingredient in these contemporary selections. Recipes range from appetizers to pizza, soups to salads. Your friends and family will welcome this untraditional approach to eating a balanced meal, whether it's dinner, lunch, brunch, snacks or informal feasts for unexpected guests.

Today's consumer's interest in nutrition for a healthy lifestyle is an integral part of the lighter style of eating. Often today a sit-down dinner or full-course meal seems inappropriate, and it is for those times I've compiled these savory selections. Many of the recipes rely upon small amounts of poultry, making them ideal for using up leftovers. Celebrate good food in the lighter style!

Peggy's Grilled Chicken Salad Chinoise, page 72

PEGGY'S GRILLED CHICKEN SALAD CHINOISE

Don't be put off by the long list of ingredients. Most of this can be done well in advance, and you'll be delighted with the simple yet elegant presentation. It took longer to write the recipe than it did to make it!

6 chicken breast halves, skinned, boned
Marinade (recipe below)
18 shiitake mushrooms (fresh, if possible)
Dressing (recipe below)
9 to 10 cups assorted greens (about 1-1/2 lbs.) such as arugula, mache, spinach leaves, watercress and radicchio
1 small bunch cilantro, broken into small sprigs, stems discarded
6 green onions, sliced diagonally into 1-inch pieces
4 ounces Chinese egg noodles, cooked, cooled and drained
24 thin asparagus spears (optional), blanched, cooled
Black sesame seeds (optional)

MARINADE:
1/4 cup light soy sauce
1/2 teaspoon kosher salt
1 teaspoon Szechuan peppercorns, toasted, then coarsely ground
1 teaspoon vermouth or dry sherry
3 quarter-size gingerroot slices, crushed with flat side of a knife
1/2 teaspoon Chinese five-spice powder
2 garlic cloves, bruised
2 teaspoons peanut oil
1/2 teaspoon sesame oil
3 drops of chile oil
1 teaspoon sugar

DRESSING:
1 tablespoon cider honey vinegar
1 tablespoon sherry wine vinegar
1/4 cup olive oil
1/2 teaspoon sesame oil
1 teaspoon kosher salt

Rinse chicken in cold water and pat dry. Make marinade, reserving 2 tablespoons for the dressing. Add chicken to marinade; marinate 30 minutes or as long as 2 hours. Remove chicken from marinade; reserve marinade for basting. Preheat gas grill or ignite charcoal and burn until flame is gone and charcoal is covered with a uniform gray ash. Grill chicken breasts, turning once, until opaque and cooked through, about 6 minutes. Grill mushrooms about 6 minutes, basting with the marinade as necessary. Cool chicken and mushrooms slightly. Make dressing. Toss greens and other vegetables and noodles with all but 3 tablespoons of dressing. Divide the salads evenly among six plates. Slice each warm chicken breast diagonally across the grain into 1/2-inch-thick slices. Use a large spatula to slide under chicken breasts to transfer to center of each salad. Crisscross asparagus spears on each side, if desired. Arrange grilled mushrooms on the side of the plates. Drizzle reserved dressing over the chicken breasts. Top each serving with a sprinkling of black sesame seeds, if desired. Makes 6 servings.

MARINADE:
Combine all ingredients in a medium-size bowl.

DRESSING:
Combine all ingredients in a small bowl.

CHICKEN BURGERS ON BRIOCHE WITH RED-ONION MARMALADE

Here's an elegant treatment for burgers. Each component of this recipe is a delicious treat in itself—so feel free to experiment with other combinations using ground turkey burgers or traditional hamburger buns. Serve burgers with a watercress salad. Cranberry Chutney (page 144) could be an alternative topping!

Brioche (page 132)
Basic Mayonnaise (page 141) to taste
Chicken Burgers (recipe below)
Red-Onion Marmalade (recipe below)

CHICKEN BURGERS:
4 to 5 chicken breast halves, skinned, boned (about 1-1/2 pounds *total*)
1 cup fresh brioche or other bread crumbs, divided in half
2 tablespoons Chicken Stock (page 23)
2 tablespoons whipping cream
2 shallots, minced
1 tablespoon chopped fresh thyme leaves or 1 teaspoon dried thyme leaves
Salt and freshly ground white pepper to taste
About 2 tablespoons vegetable oil

RED-ONION MARMALADE:
2 tablespoons olive oil
4 red onions, thinly sliced
2 tablespoons sugar
1/2 teaspoon kosher salt
3/4 cup dry red wine
1/4 cup balsamic vinegar

Slice brioche into 6 (1/2-inch-thick) slices. Reserve remainder for bread crumbs or other uses. Trim crusts or cut into 3-1/2-inch rounds using a cookie cutter. Toast, if desired. Spread a generous portion of mayonnaise on each round. Top with a Chicken Burger, then Red-Onion Marmalade. Makes 6 servings.

CHICKEN BURGERS:
Rinse chicken in cold water and pat dry. Cut chicken into 1-inch cubes. Place in a food processor fitted with the metal blade and coarsely chop. Add 1/2 cup bread crumbs, stock, cream, shallots, thyme, salt and pepper. Process to blend well and then remove and shape into 6 balls. Roll each ball in remaining 1/2 cup bread crumbs and flatten into patties, about 1/2 to 3/4 inch thick. Heat 2 tablespoons oil in a medium-size skillet. Add patties; cook 5 to 6 minutes per side over medium-low heat, adding more oil, if necessary. Makes 6 servings.

RED-ONION MARMALADE:
Heat oil in a medium-size skillet over low heat. Add onions; sauté until tender but not brown. Add sugar, salt and wine and simmer until nearly all liquid is gone, about 20 minutes. Add vinegar and cook until onions have caramelized, about 10 minutes. Serve warm or at room temperature.

VARIATION
For added flavor, you may want to grill your chicken burgers over charcoal. In that case, lightly butter the brioche rounds and grill them as well.

Herbed Pasta Salad With Chicken & Chèvre

This rich and tangy salad contains many of the flavors popular in "California Cuisine."

Basil Dressing (recipe below)
1 pound Herb Pasta (page 154) made
   with fresh basil or a combination of
   herbs or other pasta, cut into
   1/8-inch strips
2 cups cooked coarsely chopped
   chicken
1 (12-oz.) jar marinated artichoke
   hearts, drained, quartered
1/2 cup oil-packed sun-dried tomatoes,
   drained, chopped (reserve the oil, if
   possible)
12 ounces goat cheese, such as
   California Chèvre or French
   Montrachet, crumbled
1/2 cup oil-cured ripe olives, pitted,
   halved
Additional olive oil, if necessary

BASIL DRESSING:
1/2 cup basil leaves, chopped
2 tablespoons fresh lemon juice
2 tablespoons white wine vinegar
1/2 teaspoon salt
Freshly ground pepper
1/2 to 3/4 cup olive oil

Make dressing. Cook pasta as directed and drain in a colander, rinsing with cold water and draining well. In a large bowl, toss the pasta with the chicken, artichokes, tomatoes, goat cheese, olives and dressing. Adjust seasonings, if necessary. Serve immediately, or store, covered, in the refrigerator, tossing again, before serving. Makes 4 to 6 main-dish servings.

BASIL DRESSING:
In a small bowl or food processor, combine ingredients for dressing and set aside.

Curried Chicken Salad

Excellent as a sandwich filling; this can be served on lettuce as an entree. You may want to offer small bowls of traditional curry condiments, such as raisins, coconut or chutney, when serving this as your main course. Poppadums are another nice accompaniment (page 79).

3 cups cubed cooked chicken breasts
1 cup diced celery
1 tart apple, cored, diced
3 green onions, chopped
1/2 cup macadamia nuts or toasted
   almonds, coarsely chopped
Curry Mayonnaise Dressing (page 79)

In a medium-size bowl, combine the chicken, celery, apple, onions and nuts. Fold in dressing to taste. Serve immediately, or refrigerate up to 3 hours. Makes 6 servings.

CHINESE CHICKEN NOODLE SALAD

To maintain their bright colors, it is best to toss the vegetables in just before serving.

1 pound Chinese egg noodles or vermicelli, cooked, drained and rinsed with cold water
1 pound cooked chicken, cut into narrow strips
1 bunch green onions, diagonally cut into 1-inch pieces
4 celery stalks, diagonally cut into 1/4-inch pieces
1 red bell pepper, finely chopped
1 small bunch cilantro, chopped
1/4 pound snow peas, blanched
1/4 pound wild or cultivated mushrooms, sliced and sautéed quickly in 2 tablespoons peanut oil
2 ounces pine nuts or slivered almonds, toasted

DRESSING:
1/4 cup light soy sauce
1 large garlic clove, minced
1 tablespoon rice wine vinegar
3 tablespoons peanut oil
2 tablespoons sesame oil
2 teaspoons Chinese hot chile oil

TIP

Use aromatic sesame oil from oriental or Middle Eastern markets.

Mix the noodles with other ingredients. Make dressing, then toss into noodle mixture. Makes 6 to 8 servings.

DRESSING:
In a small bowl, mix dressing ingredients together.

PEGGY'S DUCK SALAD WITH WILD RICE & CURRANTS

To quickly assemble this lovely salad, purchase roast duck from a Chinese market.

1 (5-lb.) duck, cooked
3 cups cooked wild rice, cooled (made from 1 cup uncooked wild rice)
Chopped zest of 1 orange, blanched in boiling water about 2 minutes
1/3 cup currants or raisins
1/2 cup walnuts, toasted
1 small red onion, thinly sliced
Mustard Dressing (recipe below)
4 cups of mixed lettuces
Cilantro sprigs

MUSTARD DRESSING:
1 tablespoon Dijon-style mustard
1/4 cup cider honey vinegar
1/3 cup walnut oil
1/3 cup olive oil
Salt and freshly ground pepper to taste

TIPS

To get the most flavor from dried currants, "plump" them in very hot water 15 minutes and drain before adding to your recipe.
Blanching orange zest will remove any bitterness that may be present.

Preheat oven to 400F (205C). Remove meat from duck and shred into bite-size pieces. Place pieces of duck skin on a rack and heat in oven until crisp. Slice or chop skin into pieces. Mix the duck meat and skin, wild rice and orange zest with the currants, walnuts and onion. Set aside. Make dressing. Moisten salad with some of the dressing. Just before serving, toss in the lettuces and add more dressing. Adjust seasonings to taste. Garnish each serving with a few cilantro sprigs. Makes 6 servings.

MUSTARD DRESSING:
In a small bowl, mix all ingredients together.

CHINESE CHICKEN SALAD IN PITA POCKETS

These are great for either lunches or snacks.

8 pita bread rounds
6 chicken breast halves, cooked,
   skinned, boned
4 celery stalks, chopped
2 green onions, chopped
1 bunch cilantro, chopped
1/2 cup almonds or pine nuts, toasted
Asian-Style Mayonnaise (page 141)
Shredded Napa cabbage or iceberg
   lettuce
Toasted or black sesame seeds
   (optional)
Cilantro sprigs (optional)

Cut pita bread into quarters. Shred chicken. Mix shredded chicken with celery, onions, cilantro and almonds. Fold in mayonnaise to taste, and adjust seasonings, if necessary. Place shredded cabbage or lettuce in each pita. Add chicken salad. Garnish with sesame seeds and/or cilantro sprigs, if desired. Makes 8 servings.

SMOKED CHICKEN SALAD WITH HONEY & TOASTED ALMONDS

Serve this unusual treat with your favorite corn bread and Honey Butter (page 137).

Honey Vinaigrette (recipe below)
4 smoked chicken breast halves, cut
   into bite-size pieces
1/4 cup chopped green onions
1/2 cup slivered almonds, toasted
1 cup jicama, cut into 1/4-inch cubes
6 cups spinach leaves
1 large papaya, cut lengthwise into
   thin slices

HONEY VINAIGRETTE:
1 tablespoon Dijon-style mustard
1/4 cup unseasoned rice wine vinegar
2 tablespoons light soy sauce
1/4 cup honey
2 tablespoons sesame seeds, toasted
1 shallot, minced
3/4 cup peanut oil or other oil
3 drops sesame oil
Salt and freshly ground white pepper
   to taste

Make vinaigrette. In a medium-size bowl, combine chicken, onions, almonds and jicama; set aside. In a large bowl, toss spinach with a bit of vinaigrette to moisten, and divide among salad plates. Dress chicken mixture with some of the remaining dressing and place on top of spinach. Garnish with papaya slices and serve immediately. Makes 4 to 6 servings.

HONEY VINAIGRETTE:
In a small bowl, combine mustard, vinegar, soy sauce, honey, sesame seeds and shallot. Whisk in oils and season to taste. Makes about 1-1/2 cups.

SOUTHERN FRIED CHICKEN SALAD

Here's a lighter and healthier way to enjoy everyone's favorite Sunday supper, with spicy bits of boneless fried chicken on top of cool salad greens. Serve freshly made Buttermilk Biscuits (page 132) with Honey Butter (page 137) on the side.

4 chicken breast halves, skinned,
   boned
1 cup buttermilk
Plantation Dressing (recipe below)
5 cups mixed greens (preferably a mix
   of arugula, red leaf, oak leaf,
   mache, etc.)
3/4 cup coarsely chopped pecans
2 cups peanut or other oil for
   deep-frying
1 cup black-eyed peas, cooked, cooled
1 cup fresh corn, cut from about 3
   medium-size ears or 1/2 (10-oz.)
   package frozen corn, thawed
1/2 cup all-purpose flour
1 teaspoon *each* salt and coarsely
   ground black pepper
1/2 teaspoon red (cayenne) pepper

PLANTATION DRESSING:
1/2 cup Basic Mayonnaise (page 141)
1/2 cup buttermilk
1 garlic clove, minced
2 tablespoons chopped parsley
Salt and freshly ground pepper to taste
1 tablespoon grated onion
1 teaspoon tarragon vinegar
1 tablespoon chopped fresh dill weed,
   or 1 teaspoon dried dill

Preheat oven to 350F (175C). Rinse chicken in cold water and pat dry. Slice each chicken breast into 6 or 8 pieces. Place in a medium-size bowl, add buttermilk, cover and refrigerate at least 4 hours or overnight. Make dressing. Wash and dry the greens and store in the refrigerator until ready to serve. Place pecans in a baking pan; bake 10 to 15 minutes, until toasted. Set aside. Heat vegetable oil to 375F (190C) or until a 1-inch bread cube turns golden-brown in 50 seconds. Meanwhile, in a large bowl, toss greens with dressing to moisten. Divide the dressed greens equally among 4 large plates. Scatter the peas, corn and pecans over the greens. Mix flour with salt, pepper and cayenne. Drain chicken pieces; dredge in seasoned flour. Deep-fry chicken in small batches until golden-brown and cooked through, about 1 minute. Drain on paper towels and divide equally among salads. Serve immediately. Makes 4 servings.

PLANTATION DRESSING:
Mix all ingredients together in a small bowl and refrigerate at least 1 hour for flavors to blend. Dressing will keep at least 4 days in the refrigerator.

CURRIED PASTA SALAD WITH DUCK

This could be served with Nectarine Chutney (page 116) or Cranberry Chutney (page 144) on the side.

Curry Mayonnaise Dressing (recipe below)
1/2 cup bourbon whiskey or water
1/2 cup currants
Poppadums (recipe below)
3 carrots, cut into 1/8-inch-thick rounds
1 bunch green onions, finely chopped
1/2 cup slivered almonds, toasted
1 pound farfalle (butterfly or bow-tie shaped pasta), cooked *al dente* and rinsed in cold water
Meat from 1/2 roasted duck, skinned, cut into bite-size pieces

CURRY MAYONNAISE DRESSING:
2 tablespoons curry powder or to taste
1 tablespoon fresh lemon juice
1 recipe Basic Mayonnaise (page 141) or 1 cup mayonnaise and 3/4 cup dairy sour cream
1 garlic clove, minced
Dash of sugar
Salt and freshly ground white pepper to taste

POPPADUMS:
2 to 3 cups vegetable oil
1 bag or box of poppadums (approximately 20)

Make dressing. Heat whiskey in a small pan; add currants. Remove from heat and set aside 15 minutes, then drain and discard liquid. Cook poppadums. In a medium-size saucepan filled with boiling water, blanch carrot rounds 1 minute. Remove from heat, drain and rinse with cold water. Mix all ingredients together in a large bowl and toss with dressing, to taste. Pass additional dressing, if desired. Serve with poppadums. Makes 8 servings.

CURRY MAYONNAISE DRESSING:
Combine curry powder and lemon juice; stir into mayonnaise until blended. Stir in garlic, sugar, salt and pepper. Refrigerate.

POPPADUMS:
Heat oil in a wok or large skillet to 375F (190C). Using tongs, slide poppadums into hot oil one at a time. After a few seconds they will turn slightly brown and puff up. Remove from oil and drain on paper towels. Serve at room temperature or reheat at 375F (190C) 5 minutes.

Basic Pizza Dough

With a food processor and some rapid-rise yeast, making pizza at home is no longer a chore.

1 (1/4-oz.) package active dry yeast
Pinch of sugar
3/4 cup warm water (110F/45C)
2 cups all-purpose flour
1/2 teaspoon salt
About 2 tablespoons olive oil
Cornmeal

Dissolve yeast and sugar in warm water in a small bowl. Let stand until foamy, about 10 minutes.

Put flour and salt into bowl of a food processor fitted with the metal blade and process on-and-off 3 times to combine. With motor running, add yeast mixture and 2 tablespoons oil through feed tube and continue processing until mixture forms a ball and appears firm. Turn out dough on a lightly floured surface and knead by hand a few times. Lightly oil a large bowl. Place dough in the bowl, turning a few times to lightly coat with oil. Cover and let rise in a warm draft-free place until doubled in bulk, about 45 minutes. Preheat oven to 475F (245C) at least 30 minutes. Punch dough down. Turn out dough on a floured surface. Invert the bowl over the dough to cover, and rest 10 minutes before forming pizza.

Lightly oil a 15-inch pizza pan or a 17" x 11" baking sheet and dust with a little cornmeal. Roll dough to approximate shape of the pan, transfer to pan and stretch gently to fit. Arrange filling on top of dough, brushing edges with a bit more olive oil, if desired. Place on lowest shelf in an electric oven (or on the oven floor of a gas oven) and bake 12 to 15 minutes, until cheese is bubbly and crust is brown. Slide pizza onto a large cutting board or platter and allow to cool about 1 minute before slicing and serving. Makes 1 (15-inch) pizza.

To make dough by hand:
Place flour in a large bowl and make a well in the center. Pour yeast mixture into the center of the well, gradually mixing the surrounding flour into the well. When half of the flour has been mixed in, add olive oil and salt. Continue adding flour until a sticky ball of dough has formed. Turn out onto a floured surface and knead until smooth and elastic, about 10 minutes. Lightly oil a large bowl and proceed as described above.

Variations
Substitute bread flour for the all-purpose flour to make a chewier crust.
Substitute 1/4 cup whole-grain flour, such as rye or whole-wheat, for the all-purpose flour in the dough.
Add 1 to 2 tablespoons of fresh herbs (or 1 to 2 teaspoons dried) to the dough for extra flavor.

Mexicali Chicken Pizza, page 82

Mexicali Chicken Pizza

Basic Pizza Dough (page 81)
2 or 3 tablespoons olive oil
2 chicken breast halves, skinned,
   boned and cut into strips
1 small onion, chopped
1 small red or green bell pepper,
   seeded, diced
1 to 2 jalapeño chiles, seeded, minced
Salt and freshly ground pepper to taste
2 tomatoes, seeded, diced
1/4 cup chopped cilantro
1 to 2 teaspoons dried hot pepper
   flakes
1-1/2 cups shredded Monterey Jack
   cheese

Make pizza dough; let rest. In a large skillet, heat 2 tablespoons olive oil over high heat. Add chicken; quickly sear the chicken (it will cook again in the hot oven). Reduce heat to medium; add onion, bell pepper and chiles. Cook until barely softened but not browned, about 2 minutes, adding an extra tablespoon of oil, if necessary. Season with salt and pepper and remove from heat. Stir in the tomato, cilantro and dried pepper; set aside to cool. Shape pizza dough. Spread the cooled chicken mixture over the top of the pizza dough and cover with cheese. Bake according to directions in basic pizza recipe. Makes 1 (15-inch) pizza.

Hoisin Duck Pizza

Basic Pizza Dough (page 81)
2 tablespoons peanut oil
2 garlic cloves, minced
2 quarter-size pieces gingerroot,
   peeled, minced
1/4 cup chopped green onion
2 cups shredded cooked duck meat
   and skin
3 tablespoons hoisin sauce
A few drops of hot chile oil
1/4 cup chopped cilantro
1 teaspoon sesame oil

Make pizza dough; let rest. In a large wok or skillet, heat peanut oil over medium-high heat. Add garlic and gingerroot; stir-fry until fragrant. Stir in green onion, then duck meat and skin, hoisin sauce, chile oil and cilantro. Remove from heat and combine well. Shape pizza dough. Brush pizza dough with sesame oil. Turn duck mixture onto the dough and distribute evenly and bake according to directions in basic pizza recipe. Makes 1 (15-inch) pizza.

Note: Cooked duck has a tendency to dry out when reheated, so this would be an excellent way to use Duck Confit (page 30).

TUSCAN TURKEY PIZZA

Basic Pizza Dough (page 81)
6 tablespoons olive oil
8 ounces turkey sausage
4 ounces mushrooms, sliced
1 Japanese eggplant, thinly sliced
1 medium-size zucchini, thinly sliced
1/2 cup Fresh Tomato Sauce (page 138) or commercial pizza sauce
1 tablespoon minced garlic
1 tablespoon chopped fresh herbs, such as parsley and oregano or 1 teaspoon dried leaf herbs
4 ounces mozzarella cheese, shredded
2 ounces Parmesan cheese, shredded

Make pizza dough; let rest. In a large skillet over high heat, heat 1 tablespoon of the oil. Add sausage; cook until just barely cooked. Remove with a slotted spoon and add 3 tablespoons of the oil to the hot skillet. Quickly brown the mushrooms, eggplant and zucchini in separate batches, removing each batch with a slotted spoon when completed. Shape dough. Spread sauce over the dough and top with sausage, drained mushrooms, eggplant and zucchini. Top with garlic and herbs and then the cheeses. Drizzle the remaining olive oil over the top and bake as directed in basic pizza recipe. Makes 1 (15-inch) pizza.

CHICKEN & PESTO PIZZA

Basic Pizza Dough (page 81)
1 tablespoon olive oil
1 cup Basic Pesto (page 142)
2 cups cubed, cooked chicken
1/3 cup pine nuts, toasted
8 ounces mozzarella cheese, shredded

Make pizza dough and shape. Brush the dough with olive oil. Spread a layer of pesto and top with chicken and nuts. Sprinkle with mozzarella and bake according to directions in basic pizza recipe. Makes 1 (15-inch) pizza.

Barnyard Chicken & Pasta Salad In Vegetable Nests

Shredded vegetables make a colorful "nest" for this delicious pasta salad.

4 carrots
2 celery stalks
2 small zucchini
3/4 cup olive oil
1 tablespoon fresh lemon juice
Salt to taste
2 chicken breast halves, cooked,
   skinned and boned
8 ounces Creste di Gallo (pasta shaped
   like rooster's combs) or farfalle,
   boiled until *al dente,* drained and
   rinsed in cold water
1 medium-size tomato, seeded, diced
1/4 cup minced parsley
2 ounces goat cheese (such as
   Montrachet), crumbled
2 garlic cloves, minced
2 tablespoons tarragon vinegar or
   other white wine vinegar
Freshly ground pepper to taste
1 large egg, hard-cooked, diced
6 bacon slices, crisp-cooked, crumbled

Cut carrots, celery and zucchini lengthwise into matchstick-thin julienne strips (a mandoline works well for this). Place vegetables in a medium-size bowl, toss with 1/4 cup of the oil, lemon juice and a dash of salt. Cover and refrigerate at least 10 minutes. Cut chicken into cubes. In a large bowl, combine chicken, pasta, tomato, parsley and cheese. In a small bowl, mix garlic with vinegar and whisk in remaining 1/2 cup oil. Season with salt and pepper and toss with the other ingredients except vegetable strips. Drain vegetables and form loose nests on serving plates. Top with pasta salad. Garnish with hard-cooked egg and bacon and serve. Makes 4 to 6 servings.

SQUAB & FRUITED COUSCOUS SALAD

Serve this exotic salad with a crisp California Chardonnay and a loaf of rustic whole-grain bread.

1/2 cup golden raisins
1/3 cup coarsely chopped dried
    apricots
Salt and freshly ground white pepper
    to taste
2 teaspoons curry powder
1 garlic clove, minced
1 teaspoon honey mustard or
    Dijon-style mustard
1/3 cup fresh lemon juice
3/4 cup olive oil
3 squab
2 tablespoons vegetable oil
1 recipe Boiled Couscous (page 153),
    cooled to room temperature
3 celery stalks, minced
3 green onions, minced
1/4 cup minced parsley
1/3 cup chopped pistachios or lightly
    toasted pine nuts
6 cups mixed salad greens such as oak
    leaf lettuce, escarole and butter
    lettuce

If raisins and apricots are not moist and pliable, place in two small heatproof bowls, cover with boiling water and soak 15 minutes. Drain and set aside. In another small bowl, combine salt, pepper, curry powder, garlic, mustard and lemon juice. Whisk in olive oil; set dressing aside. Rinse squab with cold water and pat dry. Bone breasts from squab by cutting along the breastbone (page 13). Remove legs and reserve remaining carcass for stock or other uses. Season meat with salt and pepper. Heat 2 tablespoons oil in a large skillet over medium-high heat. Add squab breasts and legs; sauté until browned but still medium rare, about 8 minutes for breasts and 3 to 5 minutes for legs.

Meanwhile, transfer couscous to a large bowl, breaking up any lumps with a fork. Mix in celery, green onions, parsley, raisins, apricots and nuts. Toss with enough of the reserved dressing to moisten thoroughly. Distribute salad greens over six plates and top with couscous mixture. Slice cooked squab breasts on the diagonal and arrange pieces of breast and whole legs on top of couscous. Drizzle remaining dressing over squab and salad greens. Makes 6 servings.

BRANDIED PÂTÉ WITH APPLES & PISTACHIOS

This rich spread is wonderful with cocktails when served on toast points, British water biscuits or fresh apple slices. Using a food processor for all the chopping and slicing makes preparation a breeze.

1-1/2 pounds chicken livers
3/4 cup unsalted butter, divided into 3 (1/4-cup) portions
3 tablespoons vegetable oil or rendered chicken fat
2 medium-size tart apples, peeled, cored and sliced
2 medium-size onions, coarsely chopped
1/2 cup brandy
1/2 cup pistachios, coarsely chopped
2 tablespoons fresh lemon juice
Salt and freshly ground pepper to taste
1/4 teaspoon freshly grated nutmeg

Rinse chicken livers and dry well between layers of paper towels. If the livers are large, cut into pieces and set aside. In a large skillet over medium heat, melt 1/4 cup butter with oil. Add apples and onions; sauté until golden brown, taking care not to burn. Remove apples and onions with a slotted spoon and set aside. In the same skillet, melt another 1/4 cup butter over medium heat. Add chicken livers; sauté until browned on the outside yet still slightly pink inside, about 4 minutes. Remove livers from pan and add to reserved apples and onions to cool. To the same skillet over medium heat, add the brandy, using a wooden spoon to scrape up any bits which cling to the pan. Remove from heat. Add this reduced sauce to liver mixture.

In a food processor fitted with the metal blade, process the liver mixture and brandy mixture with the remaining 1/4 cup butter until the mixture is thoroughly blended, but still maintains a bit of texture. Add nuts, lemon juice, salt, pepper and nutmeg and process just to combine. Turn the mixture into a 4-cup serving terrine or bowl and cover tightly with plastic wrap. Refrigerate at least 6 hours for the flavors to blend. Remove from refrigerator at least 30 minutes before serving. Makes 3-1/2 cups.

POLENTA & CHICKEN TORTA

All this needs is a crisp green salad to round out the meal. Using charcoal grilled chicken breasts will give this hearty entree a truly remarkable flavor.

3 cups Chicken Stock (page 23), or
    commercial chicken stock

1 cup milk

1/4 cup unsalted butter

1 cup polenta

3 tablespoons chopped sun-dried
    tomatoes, drained of oil

2 ounces mozzarella cheese, shredded

1 ounce Parmesan cheese, grated

2 ounces Italian Fontina cheese,
    shredded

2 tablespoons chopped fresh basil
    leaves or 2 teaspoons dried leaf
    basil

10 Kalamata olives, pitted, diced

2 garlic cloves, minced

Salt and freshly ground pepper to taste

2 grilled or poached chicken breast
    halves, skinned, boned and cut into
    1/2-inch chunks

Tear off a piece of plastic wrap at least 16 inches long and use it to line the interior of a 9-inch-round cake pan. Set aside. Place the Chicken Stock, milk and butter in a large saucepan; bring to a boil. Add polenta in a slow, steady stream and cook, stirring constantly, 20 minutes or until the grains are tender and the mixture is creamy. Stir in all the remaining ingredients and turn the mixture into the lined cake pan. Cover top with additional plastic wrap if necessary, and refrigerate at least 1 hour or overnight. Before serving, preheat oven to 400F (205C). Pull back the plastic wrap on top of the pan. Unmold torta onto a board and peel away the remaining plastic wrap. Cut the torta into 4 to 6 wedges and place each on a heatproof plate. Reheat slices in a 400F (205C) oven 10 minutes or until heated through. Makes 6 servings.

Chicken & Apple Salad With Warm Brie Dressing & Candied Walnuts

This elegant salad is perfect for a light autumn meal. Instead of chopping the chicken and apples, you may want to slice and arrange them as a composed salad.

Candied Walnuts (recipe below)
4 chicken breast halves, cooked, skinned and boned
1 tart green apple, skin left on, cubed
1 tart red apple, skin left on, cubed
1/4 cup chopped fresh basil leaves
1 tablespoon fresh lemon juice
Warm Brie Dressing, (recipe below)
Salt and freshly ground white pepper to taste
6 cups tender spinach leaves

Warm Brie Dressing:

1/2 cup olive oil
3 large shallots, minced
1/2 cup dry white wine
2 tablespoons sherry wine vinegar
2 tablespoons Dijon-style mustard
10 ounces ripe Brie, rind removed, cut into small pieces
Freshly ground pepper

Candied Walnuts:

1/2 cup sugar
1/4 cup water
1 cup walnut halves or pieces

Candy walnuts; set aside. Cut chicken into cubes. In a medium-size bowl, mix together the chicken, apples, basil and lemon juice. Make dressing. Add enough dressing just to moisten, then season with salt and pepper. Arrange spinach on plates. Arrange salad on spinach leaves, drizzle a little more dressing over all and sprinkle with walnuts. Makes 4 to 6 servings.

Warm Brie Dressing:

Warm olive oil in a medium-size skillet over very low heat. Add shallots; cook until softened, about 3 minutes. Whisk in wine, vinegar and mustard. Add cheese and stir until smooth. Season with pepper, remove from heat and serve immediately. Makes about 2 cups.

Candied Walnuts:

In a medium-size skillet over medium heat, dissolve the sugar in the water. Increase heat to medium-high and add the nuts. Stir constantly until shiny and glazed. Spread nuts on foil to cool. Coarsely chop or break apart while still slightly warm. When completely cool, store in an airtight container. Makes about 1-1/4 cups.

CROSTINI DI FEGATINI

The subtle flavors in this Italian version of chopped liver will make it a hit at cocktail time. Serve with plenty of toasted baguette slices.

2 tablespoons unsalted butter
2 tablespoons olive oil
1/4 cup minced onion
1 pound chicken livers, rinsed
1/3 cup dry Marsala or sherry wine
2 tablespoons anchovy paste or to taste
1 (3-oz.) jar capers, drained
Coarsely ground pepper to taste

In a large skillet over medium heat, melt butter with oil. Add onion and chicken livers; cook until onion is softened but not browned, and livers are just barely cooked, about 4 minutes. Increase heat to high and pour in Marsala. When all but 1 tablespoon of wine has evaporated, remove pan from heat and pour liver mixture into a medium-size bowl. Cool 5 to 10 minutes. Using the tines of a fork, mix in anchovy paste and capers, and coarsely crush the chicken livers. Season well with pepper and pack into a crock or glass bowl for serving. Refrigerate up to 2 days, if desired. Serve at room temperature. Makes about 2 cups.

CHICKEN & CORN TAMALES

Enjoy these untraditional, low-fat tamales in the summer when fresh corn is at its peak. Leftover grilled chicken adds a delicious smoky flavor.

Salsa de Suizas (recipe below)
10 ears of fresh corn, unhusked
1 cup cornmeal
1 tablespoon baking soda
1 tablespoon salt
1 teaspoon chile powder
1/2 cup sugar
1-1/2 cups cubed, cooked chicken
2 or 3 jalapeño chiles, minced, with some of the seeds

SALSA DE SUIZAS:

3 large tomatoes, peeled, seeded, chopped and drained
1/2 cup chopped green onions
2 to 4 jalapeño chiles, minced, with some of the seeds
1 tablespoon fresh lime juice, or to taste
1 small bunch cilantro, stems discarded, leaves coarsely chopped
Salt to taste
1 cup dairy sour cream

Make salsa; cover and refrigerate. Carefully remove and reserve whole leaves from corn, discarding silk. Trim ends, if necessary, rinse with warm water and set aside to drain. Scrape corn from the cob into a blender or food processor fitted with the metal blade; puree. Add cornmeal, soda, salt, chile powder and sugar; process to combine. Transfer mixture to a bowl and stir in chicken and chiles. Lay corn husks flat, overlapping 2 or 3 if necessary, and spoon about 1/4 cup of mixture into each. Wrap envelope style and tie loosely with a thin string torn or cut from a few of the leaves. Place tamales upright on a rack and steam, covered, over a shallow layer of simmering water 1 hour, or until filling is light and spongy. Let each guest unwrap tamales, discarding the husks, and accompany with Salsa de Suizas or any other salsa, if desired. Makes about 24 (3-inch) appetizer-size tamales.

SALSA DE SUIZAS:

Combine all ingredients and taste for seasonings. Serve chilled with warm tamales.

CHICKEN QUENELLES WITH SHALLOT & RED PEPPER SAUCE

A good quenelle has a light, nearly smooth texture that almost melts in your mouth. For best results, keep the ingredients as cold as possible.

1 pound boned, skinned chicken breasts, cut in strips and well-chilled
1 teaspoon salt
A few grindings of white pepper
1/2 teaspoon freshly grated nutmeg
2 egg whites, at room temperature
2 cups (1 pint) whipping cream, chilled
4 cups water or Chicken Stock (page 23) or a combination

SHALLOT & RED PEPPER SAUCE:

3 large shallots, minced
1/4 cup white wine vinegar
1/4 cup dry white wine
2 red bell peppers, roasted, peeled and seeded
3 egg yolks, at room temperature
1/2 teaspoon Dijon-style mustard
1 cup unsalted butter, melted and very hot but not browned

TIP

Sauce can be made 1 or 2 hours in advance if kept warm in a thermos.

Rinse chicken in cold water and pat dry. In a food processor fitted with the metal blade, puree the chicken, salt, pepper and nutmeg until smooth. With the motor running, add 1 egg white. When it has been completely incorporated, add remaining egg white; process until incorporated. Push the mixture through a fine sieve into a bowl. Cover with plastic wrap and chill well. Return the mixture to the processor fitted with the metal blade and with the motor running, slowly add the cream. Chill the mixture again. Meanwhile, bring the water to a simmer. Form the quenelles into oval shapes using 2 tablespoons dipped in hot liquid. Transfer mixture from spoon to spoon, rotating it slightly each time to produce a smooth, oval quenelle. Slide quenelles into the water and cook until slightly firm to the touch, 5 to 8 minutes. Transfer to a warm serving platter. Make sauce and spoon over the quenelles. Makes 4 servings.

SHALLOT & RED PEPPER SAUCE:

Place shallots, vinegar and wine in a small non-aluminum saucepan. Reduce over medium-high heat until only 2 tablespoons of liquid remains. Set aside. In a food processor fitted with the metal blade, puree peppers. Add reduced shallot mixture, egg yolks and mustard; process until completely smooth. With motor still running, add butter in a very slow, steady stream. Serve immediately.

CHICKEN SALAD OLÉ

With a little advance preparation, this spicy salad can be assembled in just a few minutes. Serve with ice cold beer.

4 Fried Tortillas (recipe below)
3 cups cooked cubed chicken
3 celery stalks, chopped
3 green onions, chopped
3/4 to 1 cup Chili Mayonnaise (page 141)
Salt and freshly ground pepper to taste
2 tomatoes, peeled, seeded and diced
1 avocado, sliced
1 lime, quartered
8 cilantro sprigs

FRIED TORTILLAS:
4 corn tortillas
Vegetable oil

Fry tortillas. In a medium-size bowl, toss chicken with celery and onions. Add enough mayonnaise to bind together. Season to taste with salt and pepper. Place 1 fried tortilla on each salad plate, mounding one-fourth of the chicken salad in the center. Top each portion with one-fourth of the tomatoes and place one-fourth of the avocado slices to the side. Garnish each serving with a lime wedge, 2 cilantro sprigs and an extra dab of mayonnaise, if desired. Makes 4 servings.

FRIED TORTILLAS:
Pour about 1/2 inch vegetable oil in a wok or a 1-quart skillet and heat to 375F (190C). Drop in corn tortillas 1 at a time, quickly turning once with tongs until crisp. Drain on paper towels before using. These can be fried several hours in advance, if desired.

CHICKEN SALAD WITH CHEDDAR, CHIVES & WALNUTS

This rich, tangy salad is lovely served on a leaf of butter lettuce and garnished with cherry tomatoes.

Cheddar Cheese Dressing (recipe below)
3 cups diced cooked chicken or turkey
1 bunch chives, chopped (about 1/2 cup)
1/2 cup walnuts, toasted
Salt and freshly ground pepper to taste
Lettuce leaves
Shredded Cheddar cheese
Chopped green onions
Cherry tomatoes

CHEDDAR CHEESE DRESSING:
3/4 cup Basic Mayonnaise (page 141)
1/4 cup buttermilk
1/4 cup finely shredded Cheddar cheese
Dash of Worcestershire sauce
1/2 teaspoon white wine vinegar
1/8 teaspoon hot pepper sauce
Salt and freshly ground pepper to taste

Make dressing. In a large bowl, combine chicken with chives and walnuts. Add enough dressing to coat and season to taste with salt and pepper. Line salad plates with lettuce leaves; spoon salad onto lettuce. Top with Cheddar cheese and onions. Garnish with cherry tomatoes. Makes 4 to 6 servings.

CHEDDAR CHEESE DRESSING:
Combine all ingredients in a small bowl. Makes about 1-1/4 cups.

GOOSE & PORK RILLETTES

The subtle flavor of goose enlivens the taste of this French standby. Provide lots of crusty baguette slices for serving this wonderfully rich spread. This will surely be the hit of your next cocktail party.

2 goose legs
3/4 pound boneless pork butt
6 ounces pork and/or goose fat
1 cup dry white wine
1 large carrot, peeled
1 onion, peeled
2 garlic cloves, crushed
2 thyme sprigs or 1 teaspoon dried
    leaf thyme
1/2 teaspoon salt
A generous amount of freshly ground
    pepper
1 bay leaf

Rinse goose legs in cold water and pat dry. Remove skin and bones from goose legs and cut meat away from tendons. Coarsely chop goose meat, pork and fat into 3-inch pieces. Place all ingredients in a deep heavy-bottomed 3- or-more quart pan over very low heat. Cover and cook about 4 hours, or until meat is literally falling apart. Stir occasionally while cooking; check that the meat does not stick to the bottom of pot. (If it does, add a bit more wine or water.) Discard vegetables and herbs; cool at room temperature about 1 hour and then refrigerate until fat has partly congealed. Mix occasionally to combine meat and fat. Using 2 forks, shred mixture into small pieces. The mixture should have a stringy consistency with the fat well incorporated. (Meat could also be placed in the bowl of a heavy-duty mixer and shredded by using the wire whisk attachment on low speed.) Store in crocks or jars in the refrigerator up to 10 days. Bring to room temperature before serving. Makes about 3 cups.

MARLENE'S CURRIED LIVER PÂTÉ

This delicious appetizer comes to us from Marlene Levinson, a San Francisco-based food consultant and cooking teacher. The curry powder adds a very subtle flavor that may not be identified by many.

1/2 cup unsalted butter
1 medium-size onion, chopped
1 large garlic clove, minced
1 teaspoon curry powder, or to taste
1-1/2 tablespoons all-purpose flour
8 ounces chicken livers, rinsed, dried
   and coarsely chopped
1/4 cup dry white wine
1/4 teaspoon ground allspice
1/4 teaspoon salt
1/4 teaspoon freshly ground pepper
1 large egg

Preheat the oven to 350F (175C). Butter 2 heatproof (1-cup) ramekins or 1 (2-cup) ramekin. In a large skillet, melt butter over medium heat. Add onion; sauté until softened. Add garlic and curry powder and reduce heat to low. Stir in flour until well blended, about 1 minute. Add chicken livers, wine, allspice, salt and pepper. Cover skillet and cook over low heat until livers are browned. Cool 10 minutes. Place entire mixture in a blender or food processor. Process until smooth, add egg, and process once again until smooth. Pour mixture into buttered ramekin(s). Cover tightly with foil and place inside a baking pan. Pour enough hot water into the pan to reach halfway up the sides of the ramekin(s). Bake in hot water bath 30 to 45 minutes, or until the tops of the pâtés appear set when the foil is removed. Cool and refrigerate, covered, 24 hours before serving for flavors to blend. Makes about 2 cups.

CHICKEN KABOBS WITH RED PEPPER MAYONNAISE

These light and lovely appetizers are sure to please your guests. A hollowed-out bell pepper makes a colorful container for the dipping sauce.

Marinade (recipe below)
1-1/2 pounds boneless, skinned chicken breasts, cut into 3/4-inch pieces
2 to 3 bell peppers (red, yellow or green), cut into 3/4-inch pieces
Red Pepper Mayonnaise (page 141)

MARINADE:
1/2 cup fresh lemon juice
1/2 cup olive oil
Salt and freshly ground white pepper to taste

Soak 40 (6-inch) wooden skewers in warm water 1 hour or longer to prevent charring. Make marinade. Add chicken pieces to marinade; cover and marinate at least 4 hours, or overnight in the refrigerator. Preheat broiler. Drain chicken, reserving marinade, and thread 2 pieces on each skewer with 1 piece of pepper. Broil, turning once, 5 to 10 minutes or until cooked through. Brush once or twice with reserved marinade during cooking. Serve warm or at room temperature with Red Pepper Mayonnaise as a dipping sauce. Makes about 40 appetizers.

MARINADE:
Combine all ingredients in a medium-size bowl.

CHOPPED CHICKEN LIVERS

Everyone has a favorite way of preparing this appetizer, and this is mine. Serve with thin slices of good-quality rye bread.

1/4 cup rendered chicken fat (page 22) or vegetable oil
2 large onions, coarsely chopped
1 pound chicken livers, rinsed
3 large eggs, hard-cooked
Salt and freshly ground pepper to taste
1 tablespoon minced parsley

Heat fat in a large skillet over medium-high heat. Add onions; sauté until softened but not browned. Add livers and sauté, turning frequently, 4 or 5 minutes, until browned, but still pink in the center. Transfer onions, livers and pan juices to a food processor; cool about 5 minutes. Cut 2 of the eggs into quarters and add to liver mixture. Process with an on-off motion 3 or 4 times, or until well combined but still coarse. Add salt and pepper to taste. Transfer to a glass or crockery bowl. Press the remaining egg through a sieve (or chop finely by hand or machine) and sprinkle over mixture. Cover and refrigerate up to 2 days, if desired. Serve at room temperature, topped with parsley. Makes about 2 cups (8 to 10 appetizer servings).

DUCK SOUP WITH WILD RICE & MUSHROOMS

To capture a more intense flavor, use stock made from duck bones. If you only have chicken stock available, simmer duck bones in it for about two hours to leach out all of their flavor. Duck can be very fatty, so chill the strained stock thoroughly so that all fat rises to the top, leaving a fat-free stock to use as your soup base.

1/4 cup unsalted butter
6 ounces fresh mushrooms, preferably
   wild, sliced
4 shallots, minced
2 medium-size carrots, minced
1 quart Duck Stock (page 23), or
   other poultry stock
1/2 cup Madeira
About 1/2 cup wild rice, cooked
Meat from 1 (4- to 5-lb.) cooked
   duck, skin and bones reserved for
   other uses
1/4 cup chopped parsley
Salt and freshly ground pepper to taste

In a large pot over medium heat, melt butter. Add mushrooms, shallots and carrots; sauté until softened but not browned, about 5 minutes. Pour in stock and wine and bring to a boil. Reduce heat to low and simmer 10 minutes. Stir in wild rice, duck meat and parsley. Cook until heated through, about 10 minutes. Season with salt and pepper. Makes 6 servings.

Marge Poore's Sopa De Lima (Chicken & Lime Soup)

This unusual soup from the Yucatan, so simply prepared, will make a delicious addition to your repertoire.

2 whole chicken breasts
4 chicken livers
10 whole garlic cloves, peeled
1 tablespoon chopped fresh oregano or
   1 teaspoon dried oregano leaves
2 bay leaves
1 teaspoon salt
8 cups water
2 tablespoons unsalted butter
1 large onion, chopped
2 Anaheim or Poblano chiles, peeled,
   seeded and chopped
2 large tomatoes, peeled, seeded and
   chopped
Juice from 1 or 2 limes
Freshly ground black pepper to taste
16 tortillas, cut into strips and
   deep-fried in oil until crisp
1/2 onion, minced
1 jalapeño chile, minced
Wedges of fresh lime

Rinse chicken breasts and livers with cold water and pat dry. Place whole chicken breasts, livers, garlic, oregano, bay leaves and salt in a 4- or 5-quart stock pot with the water and bring to a boil over medium heat. Reduce heat to low and simmer 30 minutes. Remove chicken, livers and garlic and set aside. Strain broth through a fine sieve, skimming off any fat that rises to the top, and return to pot. Mash garlic cloves, chop chicken livers and return both to broth. Remove and discard chicken skin and bones. Shred chicken meat and return to broth over low heat. In a medium-size skillet over medium heat, melt butter. Add onion, Anaheim chiles and tomatoes; sauté until onion is softened but not browned. Add vegetables to broth and simmer another 5 minutes. Add lime juice and pepper. Place fried tortilla strips in individual bowls. Ladle soup over. Pass a bowl of chopped onion and chile along with lime wedges for garnish. Makes 8 servings.

Marge Poore's Sopa de Lima (Chicken & Lime Soup)

Turkey & Barley Soup

A hearty soup that freezes well is an ideal way to extend the enjoyment of leftover turkey.

1 cup barley
6 cups Chicken Stock (page 23), or
   Turkey Stock (page 23)
1/4 cup unsalted butter
1 large onion, diced
3 medium-size carrots, diced
4 celery stalks, diced
1 tablespoon fresh thyme leaves or 1
   teaspoon dried leaf thyme
1 bay leaf
1-1/2 pounds cooked turkey breast or
   other turkey meat, cut into bite-size
   pieces
1/4 cup chopped parsley
Salt and freshly ground white pepper
   to taste

Cook barley in 4 cups boiling salted water until tender, about 30 minutes. Drain and set aside. Heat stock in a large pot over medium heat. Melt butter in a large skillet over medium heat. Add onion, carrots and celery; sauté until softened but not browned, about 5 minutes. Add vegetables and cooking juices to warm stock and stir in thyme and bay leaf. Reduce heat to low and simmer until carrots are tender, 5 to 10 minutes. Stir in turkey, barley and parsley and simmer until heated through. Discard bay leaf. Season with salt and pepper. Makes 6 servings.

MOTHER'S CHICKEN NOODLE SOUP

This comforting soup is a meal in itself. With chicken stock in the freezer, this can be assembled in a matter of minutes.

2 quarts Poultry Stock (page 23)
1 large onion, minced
2 medium-size carrots, diced
3 celery stalks, diced
1-1/2 pounds fresh green peas, shelled, or 1 (10-oz.) package frozen peas, thawed
2 cups diced cooked chicken
4 ounces Basic Pasta Dough (page 154), cut into 1/8-inch strips, or 4 ounces dried vermicelli
Salt and freshly ground white pepper to taste
2 tablespoons minced parsley or dill weed

Bring stock to a simmer in a large pot over medium heat. Reduce heat to low and add onion, carrots and celery and simmer 10 minutes. Stir in peas, chicken and pasta and simmer until noodles are cooked through, 5 to 7 minutes. Season with salt, pepper and parsley. Makes 8 servings.

BROILING & GRILLING

In today's busy world we all appreciate recipes that can be prepared quickly. Grilling and broiling expose poultry to intense dry heat, one side at a time, quickly searing the outside and sealing the tasty juices within.

The advantages of outdoor cooking are fairly obvious. In addition to the exhilarating smells and crackling sounds, there is the convenience of advance preparation, incomparable flavor, the prospect of a cool kitchen on a warm day and the good possibility of delegating said chore to another family member or friend! But with so many high-quality indoor grills available today, grilling poultry need not be reserved for fair weather only.

Broiling is quick and efficient. Unlike charcoal grilling, broiling imparts no particular flavors of its own; this neutral high heat allows the flavor of the poultry as well as those infused by marinades to shine through. As most ovens broil at 550F (285C) it is imperative that you keep a constant watch to avoid a burned exterior and dried out meat. Broil about 4 inches from the heat source. To encourage air flow and prevent heat buildup, leave the door of an electric oven slightly ajar while broiling. Gas ovens have a built-in ventilation system, so doors can remain shut. When grilling, place poultry four to six inches above hot, well-packed coals. To prevent flare-ups caused by fat dripping onto the coals, it is best to cook poultry over indirect heat by off-setting the coals in a semicircle and placing a drip pan in the center to catch escaping fat.

Grilled Wings & Thighs with Melon Salsa, page 102; Breast of Chicken Béarnaise, page 103

The thicker the food, the greater the distance it should be from the heat source, and the longer it will take to cook.

♦

Always preheat the broiler, but not the broiling pan. Oil the pan and line the interior of the broiler pan with foil to facilitate cleanup.

♦

Trim excess fat from poultry before grilling or broiling, since fat causes flare-ups.

♦

Halved birds will cook more evenly if they are flattened so wings and drumsticks don't protrude and brown too quickly.

♦

Begin cooking by placing birds on grill or broiler pan skin-side down.

♦

Lean birds benefit from basting, but ducks contain enough fat to baste themselves.

♦

If using a barbecue sauce, do not brush it on until the last 15 minutes of cooking, otherwise the high heat will caramelize the sugars in the sauce and char the outside of the bird.

GRILLED WINGS & THIGHS WITH MELON SALSA

Serve this piquant dish with Grilled Polenta (page 153).

Melon Salsa (recipe below)
8 chicken wings
8 chicken thighs
1/4 cup olive oil
Salt and freshly ground pepper to taste

MELON SALSA:
1-1/2 cups diced casaba melon
1-1/2 cups diced honeydew melon
1-1/2 cups diced Crenshaw melon
3/4 cup chopped papaya (optional)
2 tablespoons chopped cilantro or mint
1-1/2 teaspoons minced jalapeño chile
1-1/2 teaspoons cider honey vinegar or
   cider vinegar
1-1/2 teaspoons fresh lemon juice

Make salsa. Rinse chicken in cold water and pat dry. Place the chicken pieces in a shallow ceramic or glass dish with 1 cup of the salsa and the olive oil. Marinate at least 8 hours, but preferably as long as 48 hours. Preheat gas grill or ignite charcoal and burn until flame is gone and charcoal is covered with a uniform gray ash. Remove chicken from marinade; discard marinade. Season chicken with salt and pepper. Grill 15 to 20 minutes, turning frequently, until done. Serve with remaining salsa. Makes 4 to 6 servings.

MELON SALSA:
In a large bowl, combine all ingredients. Cover and refrigerate the mixture until serving.

BREAST OF CHICKEN BÉARNAISE

For years béarnaise sauce was reserved for beef, but I think you'll love its smoky flavor with grilled chicken. Plain fresh vegetables, such as steamed asparagus and ripe, sliced tomatoes make the best accompaniment.

4 chicken breast halves, skinned,
   boned
Juice of 1 lemon
1 tablespoon olive oil
Salt and freshly ground white pepper
   to taste
Béarnaise Sauce (recipe below)
4 Garlic Croutons (page 51)
4 tarragon sprigs for garnish (optional)

BÉARNAISE SAUCE:
1/4 cup dry white wine
1/4 cup wine vinegar
2 shallots, finely chopped
1 tablespoon chopped fresh tarragon
3 egg yolks
Kosher salt and freshly ground pepper
   to taste
1/2 cup unsalted butter, diced

Béarnaise sauce can be made ahead and stored in a thermos 1 to 2 hours before serving.

Rinse chicken in cold water and pat dry. In a glass or ceramic dish, combine chicken breasts, lemon juice, olive oil, salt and pepper. Cover and marinate in the refrigerator at least 4 hours or overnight. Preheat gas grill or ignite charcoal and burn until flame is gone and charcoal is covered with a uniform gray ash. Grill or broil until just done, about 10 minutes. Meanwhile make sauce. Place each breast on a warm crouton and drizzle 1/4 cup sauce over the top. Garnish with tarragon, if desired. Makes 4 servings.

BÉARNAISE SAUCE:
In a small non-aluminum saucepan, boil wine, vinegar, shallots, and tarragon until only the solids and a syrupy mixture remain. Cool slightly. Place over very low heat; beat in egg yolks, salt and pepper. The bottom of pan should never become too hot to touch. When mixture is creamy, whisk in butter bit by bit until thick and creamy. Makes 1 cup.

VARIATION
Food Processor Béarnaise Sauce: Complete the reduction in first step above. In a food processor fitted with the metal blade, process egg yolks, salt and pepper. Add slightly cooled tarragon mixture. With processor motor running, add butter bit by bit through the feed tube until thick and creamy.

SAFFRON-BROILED SQUAB

Give your saffron-loving friends an extra treat by serving this with Saffron Rice (page 150). A stir-fry of assorted fresh and colorful vegetables would round out the meal.

6 squabs, halved
Salt and freshly ground pepper to taste
1/2 teaspoon saffron
1/4 cup fresh lemon juice

Preheat broiler. Rinse squab with cold water and pat dry. Cover a baking sheet with foil. Place the squab, skin-side down, on prepared baking sheet. Season with salt and pepper. In a small bowl, dissolve saffron in lemon juice. Spoon half over the squab, reserving the rest for later. Place squab 4 or 5 inches under broiler 5 minutes. Turn the squab skin-side up, season with salt and pepper and the remaining saffron mixture and broil another 5 minutes, or until the skin is crispy and golden-brown. Serve hot or warm. Makes 6 servings.

SHANGHAI TURKEY BUNDLES

Serve these as part of an appetizer buffet, or with rice and steamed fresh asparagus as a light meal.

8 ounces turkey cutlets, sliced about 1/4 inch thick
1 large egg white
1 teaspoon salt
1 teaspoon cornstarch
1 tablespoon Chinese fermented black beans, rinsed in a strainer under cold water, dried and minced
6 garlic cloves, minced (about 1 tablespoon)
1 tablespoon minced gingerroot
1/2 teaspoon sugar
1 tablespoon light soy sauce
1 tablespoon vermouth or white wine
About 8 green onions
1 teaspoon sesame oil

Preheat broiler. Rinse turkey in cold water and pat dry. Cut slices of turkey into pieces about 2 inch square. Place each piece of turkey between 2 sheets of waxed paper and pound with a mallet or the flat side of cleaver to a thickness of 1/8 inch or less. In a medium-size bowl, combine egg white with salt and cornstarch. Stir in turkey pieces and set aside. In a small bowl, combine black beans with the garlic, gingerroot, sugar, soy sauce and vermouth. Set aside. Cut the white part of the green onions into 2-inch lengths. Pour boiling water over the green part, then immediately rinse with very cold water and pat dry. Lay flat and slice into ribbons about 1/8 inch wide. Spread 3/4 teaspoon of the bean mixture on each slice of turkey, then lay 1 white part of a green onion on top and roll up tightly. Tie each bundle with a green onion "ribbon" and brush lightly with sesame oil. Broil about 4 inches from heat source about 3 minutes on each side until cooked through. Serve immediately. Makes 6 servings.

SPANISH CHICKEN WINGS

This creation was inspired by the wonderful tapas served in Spain. These are great for parties, but work equally well as an entree for a family dinner. Garnish with additional orange slices, if desired.

3 pounds chicken drumettes (largest section of wings)
2 teaspoons salt
A generous grinding of freshly ground pepper
Zest of 2 oranges, finely chopped
Juice of 2 oranges (about 1/2 cup total)
1/4 cup medium-dry sherry or cream sherry
2 tablespoons lemon juice (the juice of 1 lemon)
3 large garlic cloves, finely chopped
1 teaspoon dried red pepper flakes
1/2 cup olive oil

Rinse chicken in cold water and pat dry. Place the chicken wings in a shallow glass or ceramic dish and cover with all the other ingredients. Cover and marinate in the refrigerator at least 24 hours before grilling. Preheat gas grill or ignite charcoal and burn until flame is gone and charcoal is covered with a uniform gray ash. Grill about 4 inches from heat source about 15 minutes. These are best served at room temperature. Makes about 56 drumettes.

GRILLED GAME HENS WITH RHUBARB & RASPBERRY COULIS

Try this colorful springtime entree with wild rice and fresh asparagus.

Rhubarb & Raspberry Coulis (recipe
  below)
3 Cornish Game Hens, split in half
Salt and freshly ground white pepper
  to taste
1/2 cup unsalted butter, at room
  temperature
Grated zest of 2 oranges
Fresh watercress sprigs for garnish

RHUBARB & RASPBERRY COULIS:
2 pounds rhubarb stalks
1-1/2 cups sugar, or to taste
1/2 pint fresh raspberries
Grated zest of 1 orange
2 tablespoons unsalted butter
1 tablespoon orange liqueur or brandy

Make coulis. Preheat gas grill or ignite charcoal and burn until flame is gone and charcoal is covered with a uniform gray ash or preheat broiler. Rinse game hens with cold water and pat dry. Season with salt and pepper. In a small bowl, combine the butter and orange zest. Using your fingers, loosen the skin from the flesh and rub about 1 tablespoon of flavored butter underneath the skin of each hen. Dot about 1 tablespoon of remaining butter over tops of hens. Grill about 6 inches from heat, skin-side up, 10 to 12 minutes. Turn over, dot with remaining tablespoon butter and grill until juices run clear when pierced, 10 to 12 minutes. Transfer hen halves to a warm platter, drizzle pan juices over the top and garnish with watercress. When serving, spoon coulis to one side of each hen half. Makes 6 servings.

RHUBARB & RASPBERRY COULIS:
Wash rhubarb and cut into 1/2-inch pieces. Toss with sugar in a medium-size non-aluminum saucepan and set aside 30 minutes. Place saucepan over low heat and simmer until soft, 15 to 20 minutes. Stir in remaining ingredients and remove from heat as soon as butter has melted. Serve warm or at room temperature.

GRILLED CHICKEN THIGHS WITH RIPE OLIVE PESTO

Serve this tasty entree with Polenta (page 153) and colorful vegetables, such as grilled squash and/or peppers. Other pestos can be successfully substituted for this one.

16 chicken thighs
Salt and freshly ground pepper to taste
2 tablespoons chopped fresh thyme
  leaves or 2 teaspoons dried leaf
  thyme
1 garlic clove, minced
1/3 cup olive oil
2 tablespoons fresh lemon juice
Ripe Olive Pesto (page 142)

Rinse thighs in cold water and pat dry. Season with salt, pepper and thyme; place in a glass dish with the garlic and olive oil. Cover and marinate at room temperature 2 hours or overnight in the refrigerator. Preheat gas grill or ignite charcoal and burn until flame is gone and charcoal is covered with a uniform gray ash. Meanwhile, gently use your fingers to loosen the skin from the chicken flesh, creating a pocket and taking care that skin is still connected to meat. Place about 1 tablespoon of pesto in the pocket between the meat and skin, pressing skin back down again to seal. Place thighs on grill, skin-side down, and cook 15 to 20 minutes, turning carefully to keep skin intact and basting occasionally with some of the marinade. Makes 8 servings.

Turkey Paillard With Pommes Frites

Paillard refers not to a cooking method, but to a large thin slice of meat. If you don't mind negating the health benefits of this low-calorie entree, begin your meal with a Caesar salad and serve this with a mountain of Pommes Frites and Aioli (page 141) to use as a dipping sauce for both.

6 turkey breast cutlets
1/4 cup olive oil
Pommes Frites (recipe below)
Lemon wedges, for garnish

POMMES FRITES:
2 cups vegetable oil
6 baking potatoes, peeled and cut into
   3/8-inch julienne
Salt to taste

Rinse turkey in cold water and pat dry. Place each piece of turkey between 2 sheets of waxed paper and pound with a mallet or the flat side of cleaver to a thickness of 1/8 inch or less. Brush each paillard with oil, place in a dish, cover and refrigerate until ready to use. Make Pommes Frites. Preheat gas grill or ignite charcoal and burn until flame is gone and charcoal is covered with a uniform gray ash or preheat the broiler. Cook paillards 1 to 2 minutes per side or until cooked through. Garnish with lemon, if desired. Serve immediately. Makes 4 to 6 servings.

POMMES FRITES:
In a wok or other pan suitable for deep-frying, heat oil to 370F (190C) or until a 1-inch bread cube turns golden-brown in 50 seconds. Fry small batches of potatoes in oil 6 or 7 minutes until barely cooked and drain on paper towels (this can be done up to one hour before serving). When ready to serve, reheat the oil to 380F (195C) or until a 1-inch bread cube turns golden-brown in 40 seconds and fry small batches of potatoes in oil 1 or 2 minutes or until golden. Drain again on paper towels, sprinkle with salt and serve immediately. Makes 6 servings.

Classic Barbecued Chicken

It wouldn't be summer in our house without a platter of barbecued chicken and a bowl of homemade potato salad.

2 (3-lb.) chickens, cut into serving
   pieces
1-1/2 cups Barbecue Sauce I, II, or
   III (page 147)

Rinse chicken with cold water and pat dry. Preheat gas grill or ignite charcoal and burn until flame is gone and charcoal is covered with a uniform gray ash. Place chicken pieces, skin-side down, on grill, 4 to 6 inches from off-set coals. Once chicken skin has been seared, turn pieces skin-side up and grill 30 minutes, checking occasionally for flare-ups. Then begin brushing with barbecue sauce, turning chicken pieces frequently to prevent burning. Grill until chicken is cooked through, about 15 minutes more. Makes 8 servings.

GRILLED LEMON CHICKEN PAILLARDS WITH PROSCUITTO

This quick and tasty entree is wonderful with buttered Herb Pasta (page 154) made with sage. Reserve a few sprigs of fresh sage for garnish.

6 chicken breast halves, skinned, boned
6 thin proscuitto slices
6 thin Italian Fontina cheese slices
3 tablespoons unsalted butter
1 tablespoon lemon juice (juice of 1/2 lemon)
Salt and freshly ground pepper to taste
Zest of 1 small lemon (optional), finely chopped

Preheat gas grill or ignite charcoal and burn until flame is gone and charcoal is covered with a uniform gray ash or preheat the broiler. Rinse chicken in cold water and pat dry. Place each breast half between sheets of waxed paper and pound with a mallet or the flat side of a cleaver to a thickness of about 1/8 inch. Trim proscuitto and cheese slices to fit the size of chicken breasts and set aside. In a small saucepan over medium-low heat, melt butter with lemon juice and brush on chicken breasts. Season with salt and pepper. Grill or broil on uncoated side about 1 minute. Turn the chicken and top each piece with a proscuitto slice and then a cheese slice. Grill or broil until cheese has melted, about 2 minutes. Sprinkle with lemon zest, if desired, and serve immediately. Makes 4 to 6 servings.

ASIAN GRILLED PHEASANT BREAST

This unusual and low-calorie appetizer is sure to be a hit with your guests. You may wish to double the marinade so you can marinate and grill the pheasant drumsticks for another meal.

2 whole breasts from 2 (2-1/2-lb.) pheasants, boned
3 large garlic cloves, peeled, minced
3/4 cup sesame paste (available in Asian markets)
1/3 cup brewed black tea, strained
1/4 cup soy sauce
1 tablespoon chile oil
2 tablespoons sesame oil
2 tablespoons brown sugar
2 tablespoons rice vinegar
1/2 cup minced green onions
2 tablespoons chopped fresh cilantro, plus extra sprigs for garnish

Rinse pheasant with cold water, pat dry and place in a medium-size glass or ceramic dish. Mix remaining ingredients except cilantro together. Pour over meat, cover and refrigerate overnight. Preheat gas grill or ignite charcoal and burn until flame is gone and charcoal is covered with a uniform gray ash or preheat broiler. Grill pheasant until just cooked through, about 5 minutes per side, brushing with reserved marinade. Do not overcook. Remove from grill and rest at least 10 minutes. Cut pheasant into bite-size pieces about 1 inch square, spear with skewers and arrange on a serving platter. Garnish with cilantro sprigs. Makes 4 to 6 servings.

GRILLED DUCK BREASTS WITH PEARS & PORT VINAIGRETTE

Serve this sophisticated combination with assorted greens, crumbled blue cheese and toasted walnuts, tossed in the same warm vinaigrette.

Port Vinaigrette (recipe below)
4 duck breast halves, boned
2 slightly underripe pears, halved,
    peeled
Coarsely ground pepper to taste

PORT VINAIGRETTE:
3 medium-size shallots, minced
1 tablespoon Dijon-style mustard
1 tablespoon chopped fresh thyme or
    1 teaspoon dried leaf thyme
1/2 cup Tawny port
1/4 cup raspberry vinegar
2 tablespoons honey or maple syrup
2 tablespoons fresh orange juice or
    lemon juice
2 cups olive oil
1/2 cup walnut oil
Salt and freshly ground pepper to taste

Make vinaigrette. Rinse duck with cold water and pat dry. Marinate the duck breasts in a glass or ceramic dish with 1/2 cup of the vinaigrette, 2 hours at room temperature or overnight in the refrigerator. Preheat gas grill or ignite charcoal and burn until flame is gone and charcoal is covered with a uniform gray ash. Use the tines of a fork to prick the skin without piercing the flesh. Sear the breasts about 2 minutes on each side. Cover the grill and continue cooking another 10 to 15 minutes, turning occasionally, until done. The flesh should be pink and juicy. Heat about 1/2 cup of the vinaigrette in a small saucepan set on the grill. Use an additional 1/4 cup of the vinaigrette to baste the pears, cooking them 5 to 7 minutes until tender when pierced with a skewer. Top each cooked breast with 2 tablespoons of warm vinaigrette. Make 4 to 6 vertical slices in the wide portion of each pear half and fan them out next to the duck. Season with pepper. Makes 4 servings.

PORT VINAIGRETTE:
In a medium-size bowl, mix together the shallots, mustard, thyme, port, vinegar, honey and juice. Whisk in the oils and season with salt and pepper. Serve warm or at room temperature. Leftover dressing lasts several weeks in the refrigerator. Makes about 3 cups.

PEGGY'S CHICKEN ALLA DIAVOLA

Contrary to its name, this dish is not really as "hot as the devil"—but it's certainly one of our favorites. This makes perfect picnic fare, as it is just as delicious hot off the grill as it is when served at room temperature.

3 pounds chicken parts
1/2 cup fresh lemon juice
2 teaspoons dried red pepper flakes
2 teaspoons salt
2 teaspoons freshly cracked black
    peppercorns
2 large garlic cloves, finely minced
1/2 cup olive oil

Rinse chicken in cold water and pat dry. Combine all ingredients for marinade in a glass or ceramic pan or bowl. Add chicken, cover and marinate in the refrigerator 24 to 48 hours, turning occasionally. (This long marination is essential for the flavor.) Preheat gas grill or ignite charcoal and burn until flame is gone and charcoal is covered with a uniform gray ash. Grill chicken until done, about 20 minutes for white meat and 25 minutes for dark meat, brushing periodically with the marinade. Makes 6 servings.

BUTTERFLIED SQUAB WITH ORANGE & ROSEMARY

Since squab grills so quickly, Bruschetta (page 149) makes an ideal choice to serve with this light and flavorful entree. Keep squab warm on a platter while you toss the salad and grill the Bruschetta.

4 large garlic cloves, minced
Juice of 1 orange (about 1/2 cup)
Zest of 1 orange, finely chopped
1 tablespoon chopped fresh rosemary,
   or 1 teaspoon dried rosemary
1 teaspoon paprika
Salt and freshly ground pepper to taste
3/4 cup olive oil
6 squabs (about 6 lbs. *total*)

TOSSED GREENS WITH GORGONZOLA & TOASTED WALNUTS:

1 small head bitter lettuce such as
   escarole or frisée
1 head red leaf or butter lettuce
1 cup (4 oz.) toasted coarsely chopped
   walnuts
3 tablespoons sherry wine vinegar
3 tablespoons red wine vinegar
1 tablespoon balsamic vinegar
2 shallots, chopped
Salt and freshly ground pepper to taste
1/3 cup walnut oil
3/4 cup olive oil
8 ounces Gorgonzola cheese, crumbled

In a large bowl, combine garlic, orange juice and zest, rosemary, paprika, salt, pepper and olive oil and set aside. Rinse squab and pat dry with paper towels. Set squabs breast-side-down on a cutting board. With poultry shears or a sharp knife, cut squab lengthwise down the backbone from neck to tail. Turn over, spreading squab flat with the skin-side up. Using your fist or a heavy cleaver, strike breastbone firmly to flatten and place the squab in the reserved marinade. Repeat with remaining squab. Add to garlic mixture; marinate in the refrigerator at least 4 hours or as long as 2 days, turning occasionally in the marinade. Remove squab from refrigerator at least 1 hour before grilling. Preheat gas grill or ignite charcoal and burn until flame is gone and charcoal is covered with a uniform gray ash. Remove squab from marinade, saving the marinade remaining in the bowl. Use paper towels to pat excess marinade from squab and grill over medium-hot coals, turning as needed, until browned on both sides, a total of 12 to 15 minutes. The breast meat should still be slightly pink. Place 1 squab in the center of each of 6 plates. Place a ring of salad around the squab and scatter cheese over the lettuce. Makes 6 servings.

TOSSED GREENS WITH GORGONZOLA & TOASTED WALNUTS:

Wash lettuces and tear into bite-size pieces and spin dry. In a large bowl, toss lettuces with walnuts. In a small bowl, combine the vinegars, shallots, salt and pepper. Whisk in the oils. Add half of the dressing to the salad; toss. Gradually add as much dressing as needed to coat the lettuce leaves without saturating them (any extra dressing can be stored in the refrigerator). Cheese can be tossed in or added at the table. Makes 6 servings.

ENTERTAINING

There is no more personal way to express yourself than through entertaining in your own home. This can involve a spectacular dinner for the boss served in your formal dining room, or a potluck for friends in your studio apartment. The overall ambience and your selection of tableware, whether formal or just plain fun, all contribute to your guest's comfort and enjoyment. But long after the thank you notes have been written, the food is what we all seem to remember—for better, or sometimes, for worse.

Those of us who love to spend a leisurely day in the kitchen will find recipes in this chapter to satisfy that particular craving. For those who love the idea of entertaining, but can barely find the time to shop for groceries, let alone cook, there are some real time savers. And for the silent majority who would really rather spend Saturday night sitting in a restaurant, there are ideas for make-ahead dishes that will give you an evening of relaxed conversation rather than frantic cooking. Poultry is an ideal choice for entertaining, as it is probably the most universally accepted entree. And you needn't limit yourself to dinner parties; breakfast and luncheon invitations are usually a welcome relief in people's busy schedules.

Cook for your friends as you'd like them to cook for you. Don't feel that you always need to produce some labor-intensive extravaganza when a properly grilled chicken would be consumed with equal gusto. And who would ever object to a turkey dinner in February?

Duck with Peppercorns & Port Sauce, page 112

DUCK WITH PEPPERCORNS & PORT SAUCE

A variation on Chef Bradley Ogden's Crisp Peppered Duck served at the Campton Place Hotel in San Francisco, this spicy dish is ideal for company. Although you must begin preparation two days in advance, it need only be reheated for serving.

2 Long Island ducklings (about 5 lbs.
    each)
1/2 cup coarsely cracked black
    peppercorns, or a combination of
    black, white and pink peppercorns
Port Sauce (recipe below)
2 tablespoons kosher salt
2 large garlic cloves, chopped
2 tablespoons chopped fresh sage
    leaves, or 2 teaspoons dried leaf
    sage
1-1/2 tablespoons paprika
1 orange, cut in half
1 small onion, cut in half

PORT SAUCE:

4 prunes, or other dried fruit, cut into
    thin strips
1 cup Tawny port
2 cups Duck Stock (page 23)
2 tablespoons sugar
Juice of 1 orange
1 tablespoon cornstarch mixed with 1
    tablespoon port
Zest of 1 orange, finely chopped

TIP

To crack large quantities of peppercorns, use a mini food processor according to manufacturer's directions, or grind in an old coffee mill or spice mill cleaned and reserved only for peppercorns or crush the peppercorns beneath a heavy-duty pot.

If using frozen ducks, thaw overnight in the refrigerator. Reserve necks and giblets for another use; rinse ducks in cold water. Pat dry inside and out with paper towels. Spread the cracked peppercorns on a cutting board and roll the ducks in the pepper, pressing the pepper into the skin, until well coated. Place the ducks on a wire rack over a baking sheet or roasting pan and refrigerate, *uncovered,* 48 hours. (This technique of dehydrating the duck ensures crisp skin.) Soak prunes for sauce (see below). Preheat oven to 350F (175C). In a small bowl, combine the salt, garlic, sage and paprika into a paste. Rub the cavity of each duck with this mixture. Place half an orange and half an onion in the cavity of each duck. Place ducks on a rack in a roasting pan and cook 2 hours, or until juices run clear when duck is pierced, removing accumulated fat from the roasting pan with a bulb baster 2 or 3 times. Remove from oven and set aside until cool enough to handle. Finish sauce. Cut ducks into serving pieces (page 19). Discard carcasses or save for stock (page 23).

At this point, you could cover and refrigerate. To reheat, place duck pieces on a parchment-lined baking sheet and reheat 10 minutes at 450F (230C) before serving. For even crisper skin, place under the broiler about 2 minutes. Ladle a little sauce on each dinner plate and place a duck piece on top. Makes 4 servings.

PORT SAUCE:
Soak the prunes in the port 4 hours or overnight. Reserving the wine, remove the prunes and set aside. Simmer the wine and stock until reduced to 2 cups. Add the sugar, orange juice and cornstarch mixture and simmer together about 5 minutes or until slightly thickened. Stir in the zest and prunes.

TURKEY SAUSAGE FRITTATA

Feature this versatile dish as the entree for any brunch or lunch, or cut into small squares for an appetizer. Serve either hot or at room temperature; this creation is bound to delight your friends.

2 tablespoons olive oil
1 medium-size onion, finely chopped
1 bunch Swiss chard, leaves and stems
  chopped separately
8 ounces turkey sausage
1 pound zucchini, shredded
1 tablespoon kosher salt
2 tablespoons unsalted butter
4 ounces fresh mushrooms, sliced
1 medium-size red bell pepper,
  chopped
2 large garlic cloves, minced
6 large eggs
6 ounces Parmesan cheese, freshly
  grated (about 1-1/2 cups)
1/2 cup chopped Italian parsley

Preheat oven to 325F (165C). Butter a 9-inch-square baking dish. Set aside. Heat oil in a large skillet over medium heat. Add onion and chard stems; sauté until softened but not browned, about 1 minute. Add the sausage; use a spoon to break it into small chunks as it cooks. Once the sausage is no longer pink and has browned on the edges, use a slotted spoon to remove sausage and vegetables. Cool slightly. Discard cooking oil but reserve skillet. In a medium-size sieve placed over a bowl, toss the shredded zucchini with salt and let drain while preparing the other ingredients.

Once again using the large skillet, melt the butter, add mushrooms and sauté briefly over high heat, then toss in the bell pepper and garlic just to soften, about 1 minute. Remove from skillet with a slotted spoon and cool slightly. In a large bowl, lightly beat eggs; add cheese, parsley, reserved chard leaves and the cooked sausage mixture. Squeeze the zucchini to remove all excess liquid and add to the egg mixture. Gently stir in the mushroom mixture; pour into the prepared baking pan. Bake 40 to 45 minutes, until set and a skewer inserted into the center comes out clean. Cut into squares. Makes 4 to 6 servings.

BRAISED PHEASANT NORMANDY

This appears extravagant but is really quite simple to prepare. Wild rice cooked with mushrooms is a perfect accompaniment.

1 pheasant (2-1/2 to 3 lbs.)
Salt and freshly ground white pepper
  to taste
2 thyme sprigs or 2 teaspoons dried
  thyme leaves
1/2 cup unsalted butter
1/4 cup apple brandy
1 medium-size onion, thinly sliced
6 medium-size tart apples, such as
  Pippins, peeled
1/4 cup whipping cream

Preheat oven to 350F (175C). Rinse pheasant with cold water, pat dry and season inside and out with salt and pepper. Tuck 1 thyme sprig, or sprinkle 1 teaspoon dried thyme, into cavity and truss. In a large non-aluminum skillet over medium heat, melt 1/4 cup of the butter. Add pheasant; sauté until browned on all sides. Set pheasant aside and discard cooking fat. Return skillet to medium heat and deglaze with brandy, scraping up any browned bits which cling to the bottom of the skillet. When brandy has reduced to about 2 tablespoons, add remaining 1/4 cup butter. Add onion; cook until softened. Cut each apple into 8 to 12 slices and toss with onions. Stir in cream and remaining thyme and remove from heat. Spoon half the apple mixture into an ovenproof dish. Add pheasant and top with remaining apple mixture. Cover and bake 30 minutes, or until pheasant is tender and cooked through. Makes 2 or 3 servings.

CHICKEN THIGHS WITH PINOT NOIR & PANCETTA

Most delicatessens carry pancetta, the Italian unsmoked bacon. If using fresh thyme, garnish with additional thyme sprigs.

8 chicken thighs
2 tablespoons unsalted butter
8 ounces chanterelles or other mushrooms, sliced
2 tablespoons olive oil
8 ounces pancetta, cut into 1/4-inch cubes
1 medium-size onion, thinly sliced
1 teaspoon sugar
1 tablespoon all-purpose flour
1/2 cup Pinot Noir or other dry red wine
1/4 cup Chicken Stock (page 23)
Salt and freshly ground pepper to taste
1 tablespoon chopped fresh thyme leaves or 1 teaspoon dried leaf thyme

Rinse chicken in cold water and pat dry. In a large skillet over medium-high heat, melt butter. Add mushrooms; quickly sauté until softened but not browned, about 3 minutes. Remove with a slotted spoon and set aside; discard cooking juices or reserve for other uses. In the same skillet over medium-high heat, heat olive oil. Add pancetta; sauté until slightly crispy, about 4 minutes. Remove pancetta with a slotted spoon and drain on paper towels. In the same skillet over medium-high heat, sauté onion in oil and pancetta drippings. Stir in sugar to caramelize the onion. Remove browned onions with a slotted spoon and set aside.

Place chicken thighs in same skillet, skin-side down, and cook over medium-high heat until juices run clear when pierced, about 10 minutes. Remove chicken with a slotted spoon and discard all but 1 tablespoon cooking fat. Stir in flour and blend well with the fat over medium heat about 2 minutes or until flour is golden. Whisk in wine and stock; cook, whisking, until blended and slightly thickened, about 4 minutes. Return mushrooms, onion, pancetta and chicken to the sauce and coat well. Season with salt, pepper and thyme. Makes 4 servings.

Ragout Of Chicken Drumsticks With Ratatouille

The flavors of southern France shine through in this chicken and vegetable stew. Serve warm or at room temperature with lots of crusty bread.

1 cup all-purpose flour
1 teaspoon salt
1/2 teaspoon freshly ground black pepper
1 teaspoon paprika
16 chicken drumsticks (about 4 lbs. total)
1 cup olive oil
1 pound onions, cut into 1/2-inch slices
1 pound bell peppers, cut into 3/4-inch pieces (preferably a mixture of red, green and yellow)
1 large eggplant, cut into 3/4-inch cubes
1 teaspoon salt
Dash of red (cayenne) pepper
8 large garlic cloves, minced
2 pounds tomatoes, peeled, seeded and coarsely chopped, or 2 (15-1/2-oz.) cans whole tomatoes, drained
1 pound small zucchini, cut into 1/2-inch pieces
1 Bouquet Garni (page 21)
1/4 cup finely chopped Italian parsley
2 tablespoons chopped fresh basil leaves or 2 teaspoons dried leaf basil

Combine flour, salt, pepper and paprika in a shallow bowl. Rinse drumsticks in cold water and pat dry. Dredge in seasoned flour. Heat 1/4 cup of the olive oil in a large skillet over medium heat. Add drumsticks in several batches; sauté until browned on all sides. As they are done, transfer to a dish and set aside. Heat 1/2 cup of the olive oil in a large heavy skillet or dutch oven over medium heat. Add onions; sauté until softened but not browned. Add bell peppers, eggplant, salt and cayenne. Cook gently over medium heat 10 minutes, stirring occasionally. Add garlic, tomatoes, zucchini, Bouquet Garni and the reserved chicken. Reduce heat to low, partially cover and simmer gently 1 hour.

Use a slotted spoon to remove chicken drumsticks to a rimmed platter. Using the same slotted spoon, remove vegetables to a sieve placed over a bowl and press lightly to remove juices. Pour juices back into skillet and place vegetables into bowl and set aside. Over high heat, reduce cooking juices until about 2/3 cup of fairly thick syrup remains in pan. Remove from heat; stir in the remaining 1/4 cup olive oil and parsley and basil. Combine sauce with reserved vegetables and spoon them around the mound of chicken drumsticks. Makes 8 servings.

Gingered Duck Legs With Nectarine Chutney

The richness of duck is complemented by the sharp pungent flavor of ginger. Serve this with Boiled Couscous (page 153) and Nectarine Chutney (recipe below).

Nectarine Chutney (recipe below)
6 duck drumsticks and thighs
1 teaspoon salt
1/2 teaspoon freshly ground white
    pepper
1 (12-oz.) can ginger ale or 1-1/2 cups
    ginger beer
3 (1-inch-thick) gingerroot pieces,
    peeled, crushed

NECTARINE CHUTNEY:
1 cup packed light brown sugar
1/2 cup cider-honey vinegar or
    apple-cider vinegar
4 or 5 nectarines (about 1-1/2 lbs.
    total), unpeeled, diced
1 cup raisins
1 lemon, halved, seeded and chopped
    (with skin)
2 tablespoons chopped peeled
    gingerroot
1 large garlic clove, minced
1/8 teaspoon red (cayenne) pepper
Dash of salt

Make chutney. Rinse duck with cold water and pat dry. Place duck in a stainless steel or glass bowl; add remaining ingredients. Cover and marinate in the refrigerator 4 hours or overnight. Preheat oven to 425F (220C). Reserve the marinade and place the duck on a rack in a roasting pan and roast 40 minutes or until juices run clear when duck is pierced, basting every 5 minutes with some of the marinade. Makes 6 servings.

NECTARINE CHUTNEY:
Dissolve sugar in vinegar and bring to a boil in a medium, non-aluminum saucepan over medium-high heat. Add nectarines, raisins, lemon, gingerroot, garlic, cayenne and salt; boil 2 minutes. Remove from heat and cool. Store, tightly covered, in refrigerator or freezer. Serve at room temperature or slightly chilled. Makes about 1 quart.

Turkey Scallops With Lime-Ginger Beurre Blanc

Garnish this piquant entree with wedges of fresh lime, if desired. Steamed rice or a creamy risotto would make a nice accompaniment.

8 turkey cutlets (about 1-1/2 lbs.)
Salt and freshly ground white pepper
   to taste
3 tablespoons unsalted butter
3 tablespoons olive or vegetable oil

LIME-GINGER BEURRE BLANC:
Zest of 3 limes
2 tablespoons chopped peeled
   gingerroot
2 tablespoons chopped shallots
1/4 cup freshly squeezed lime juice
   (about 2 limes)
1/2 cup Pineau de Charente or white
   vermouth
1/4 cup pear vinegar or other fruit
   vinegar
1 cup frozen unsalted butter, cut into
   16 tablespoons

Rinse turkey in cold water and pat dry. Season with salt and pepper. Melt butter with oil in a large skillet over medium-high heat. Add turkey; quickly sauté turkey on both sides until cooked through, about 2 minutes total. Remove turkey to a warm platter and make sauce. Spoon the sauce over turkey and serve immediately. Makes 8 servings.

LIME-GINGER BEURRE BLANC:
Place all ingredients except butter in a small saucepan. Boil over medium-high heat until reduced to about 1/2 cup liquid. Strain and discard solids and return liquid to the warm saucepan. Over very low heat, whisk in butter 1 tablespoon at a time, fully incorporating each addition before adding more butter. Serve immediately.

Chicken Mousse

This ethereal classic can be piped onto canapés, used as an appetizer spread, molded for a buffet, or sliced and served as a first course or luncheon dish. Serve slices on a leaf of butter lettuce, garnished with a rosette of homemade mayonnaise, such as the Herb Mayonnaise (page 141).

4 cups diced poached chicken breasts,
   skin removed
1 tablespoon minced fresh tarragon or
   1 teaspoon dried leaf tarragon
1 teaspoon salt
Freshly ground white pepper to taste
1 (1/4-oz.) envelope unflavored gelatin
   (1 tablespoon)
1/4 cup dry white wine
2 cups warm Chicken Stock (page 23)
1 cup (1/2 pint) whipping cream
1/4 cup Basic Mayonnaise (page 141)

Finely chop chicken with tarragon, salt and pepper in a food processor fitted with the metal blade. Do not remove from the bowl. Combine gelatin in a small bowl with wine; let stand until softened. Stir gelatin mixture into the warm stock until dissolved. With the motor running, gradually pour the gelatin mixture into the chicken mixture and puree until smooth. Refrigerate this base until cool but not firm, about 10 minutes. Meanwhile, in a medium-size bowl, whip cream until stiff peaks form. Fold about 1/3 of the cream into the chicken mixture to lighten it. Then fold in the Mayonnaise and remaining cream just until combined thoroughly. Lightly oil and pour into 12 (1/2-cup) molds or 1 (6-cup) mold. To unmold, dip each mold in hot water a few seconds, loosen with the tip of a knife and invert on a plate. Makes 12 luncheon entrees, more as an appetizer.

CHICKEN TERRINE

As part of a cocktail buffet this will easily serve 25 people, but it is also a great entree for a dozen friends at a picnic, served along with Dijon-style mustard, cornichons, Niçoise olives and baguette slices. A French-style potato salad is the perfect accompaniment.

8 ounces wafer-thin bacon slices
2 tablespoons unsalted butter
1 medium-size onion, chopped
3 large garlic cloves, minced
1 (3-lb.) chicken
1/4 cup Cognac or brandy
1 pound ground veal
1/4 pound ground pork
1 tablespoon chopped fresh thyme
   leaves or 1 teaspoon dried leaf
   thyme
1/4 cup chopped Italian parsley
2 teaspoons salt
1/2 teaspoon coarsely ground pepper
1/4 teaspoon Quatre Épices or ground
   allspice
1/3 cup pistachios (optional)
1/4 cup whipping cream
2 large eggs, lightly beaten
3 bay leaves

TIP

If you prefer to eliminate the smoky flavor of the bacon, simmer it in boiling water about 10 minutes and drain before lining the terrine.

Preheat oven to 325F (165C). Line bottom and sides of a 2-quart terrine or loaf pan with half of the bacon slices and set aside. In a medium-size skillet over medium-low heat, melt butter. Add onion and garlic; sauté until softened but not browned. Set aside to cool. Rinse chicken in cold water and pat dry. Remove skin, bones and giblets and reserve for other uses. Cut breast meat lengthwise into 1/4-inch strips and marinate in Cognac while you proceed with recipe. Remove rest of meat from the chicken and chop coarsely by hand or in a food processor fitted with the metal blade. In a large bowl, combine chopped chicken, veal, pork, and onion mixture, including the butter in the skillet. Mix in thyme, parsley, salt, pepper, Quatre Épices and pistachios, if desired. Drain chicken strips, adding the Cognac marinade to the meat mixture along with cream and eggs. Combine well with your hands or a wooden spoon, then spread half into the bacon-lined terrine, packing in firmly with the back of a spoon. Lay chicken strips over meat, then cover with remaining ground meat, once again packing well. Top with reserved bacon slices and bay leaves, left whole and pressed decoratively onto the bacon. Cover terrine tightly with its lid or a double thickness of foil.

Place covered terrine inside a rectangular baking pan and fill with enough hot water to come halfway up the sides. Bake 1-1/2 hours, checking occasionally that the water has not evaporated. When done, an instant-read thermometer inserted into the center will register 165F (75C). Remove terrine from its water bath. Evenly distribute 1 to 2 pounds of weight, such as cans of food, on top of the foil to pack down meat mixture. Cool to room temperature, then refrigerate, with weights intact, at least 12 hours or as long as 3 days before serving. Makes 12 servings.

CHICKEN & MUSHROOMS IN PUFF PASTRY

In this recipe only the top of the chicken is covered with puff pastry. Press the edges of the pastry beneath the chicken so that it will adhere while baking.

You'll need only half of the recipe for the Mushroom Duxelles, but it's such a delicious treat with cocktails, you'll probably want leftovers. For a quick appetizer, spread Mushroom Duxelles on baguette slices, top with a bit of Parmesan cheese and bake at 400F (205C) until bubbly.

Mushroom Duxelles (recipe below)
8 chicken breast halves, skinned,
   boned
Vegetable oil
Salt and freshly ground white pepper
   to taste
1 (17-1/4-oz.) package frozen puff
   pastry sheets, thawed
Egg wash made from 1 egg and 1
   tablespoon whipping cream

MUSHROOM DUXELLES:

1/4 cup unsalted butter
3 tablespoons finely chopped shallots
8 ounces fresh mushrooms, finely
   chopped
2 tablespoons all-purpose flour
1/2 cup whipping cream
1/2 teaspoon salt
1/8 teaspoon red (cayenne) pepper
1 tablespoon finely chopped parsley
2 tablespoons finely chopped chives
1/2 teaspoon fresh lemon juice

Make duxelles. Refrigerate until needed. Rinse chicken in cold water and pat dry. Season chicken with salt and white pepper. Heat oil in a large skillet over medium heat. Add chicken; sauté until about three-fourths cooked, 5 minutes. Cool completely, preferably in the refrigerator. To assemble: Pat excess moisture from each chicken breast. Place 1 tablespoon of chilled Mushroom Duxelles on top of each. Divide each puff pastry sheet into 6 rectangles, rolling out larger if necessary. Wrap the chicken in the pastry, covering the Mushroom Duxelles and tucking the pastry under the chicken pieces. Brush with egg wash and place on a parchment paper lined baking sheet. Garnish with the leftover scraps of puff pastry and glaze again. Cover and refrigerate at least 30 minutes or overnight. To bake: Preheat oven to 400F (205C). Take chilled chicken directly from the refrigerator and glaze again. Bake 20 to 30 minutes, until pastry is puffed and golden. Makes 8 servings.

MUSHROOM DUXELLES:

Melt butter in a medium-size skillet. Add shallots and cook slowly until softened but not browned. Stir in mushrooms. Cook over medium heat, stirring occasionally, until all moisture has evaporated, 10 to 15 minutes. Sprinkle flour over mushrooms. Cook, stirring, 1 to 2 minutes. Pour cream into pan. Cook, stirring, until mixture boils. Remove from heat. Stir in salt, cayenne, parsley, chives and lemon juice. Makes about 1 cup.

STUFFED TURKEY THIGHS

This entree roasts leisurely in the oven while you enjoy time with your friends and family. Everyone will welcome the traditional flavors of Thanksgiving dinner captured in this unusual presentation. Serve with Wild Mushroom Ragout (page 148). Leftovers make wonderful sandwiches the next day.

4 large turkey thighs
Salt and freshly ground pepper to taste
4 tablespoons unsalted butter
1 small onion, finely chopped
2 garlic cloves, minced
1 bunch spinach, coarsely chopped
1/2 cup chopped parsley
1-1/2 teaspoons chopped fresh
   marjoram or 1/2 teaspoon dried leaf
   marjoram
1-1/2 teaspoons chopped fresh thyme
   or 1/2 teaspoon dried leaf thyme
1/4 teaspoon freshly grated nutmeg
1 large egg, lightly beaten
1/2 cup coarse fresh bread crumbs
1/2 cup (1-1/2 oz.) freshly grated
   Parmesan cheese
1/2 cup dry white wine

Preheat oven to 350F (175C). Rinse turkey in cold water and pat dry. Using a sharp boning knife or paring knife, cut through fleshy underside of thighs to expose and remove bone, taking care not to damage skin. With a mallet or flat side of a cleaver, flatten boned thighs until about 1/4 inch thick. Season with salt and pepper and set aside. Melt 2 tablespoons of the butter in a large skillet over medium heat. Add onion; sauté until softened but not browned. Add the garlic and spinach; sauté just until spinach is wilted. Remove from heat and cool slightly. Transfer the spinach mixture to a medium-size bowl and add the parsley, marjoram, thyme, nutmeg, egg, bread crumbs, cheese, salt and pepper. Divide this mixture among the thighs. Fold the thighs to enclose the filling, bringing the flaps of skin together. Secure with skewers or tie with string. Place in a shallow baking dish; cover loosely with foil. Bake 1 hour.

Meanwhile, melt remaining butter in a small saucepan; add wine. Remove foil from turkey and roast 1 hour longer, basting generously 3 or 4 times with the wine mixture. When the meat is tender and the skin is nicely browned, remove from oven and rest 10 minutes. Remove skewers and strings and slice diagonally into serving pieces. Serve 2 or 3 slices to each guest. Makes 6 servings.

Stuffed Turkey Thighs, above; Wild Mushroom Ragout, page 148

CHICKEN BREASTS PEPERONATA

Perfect for an alfresco luncheon, this colorful dish can be prepared two days in advance and refrigerated. For the best flavor, allow time to return to room temperature before serving.

6 chicken breast halves, skinned,
  boned
Salt and freshly ground white pepper
  to taste
1/4 cup olive oil
3 large garlic cloves, minced
1 large onion, thinly sliced
3 bell peppers, preferably a
  combination of red and yellow, cut
  lengthwise into 1/4-inch strips
2 tablespoons balsamic vinegar or
  sherry wine vinegar
3 tomatoes, peeled, seeded, coarsely
  chopped, or 1 (15-oz.) can
  tomatoes, drained
1/2 teaspoon sugar, if using canned
  tomatoes
Salt and freshly ground black pepper
  to taste
2 tablespoons capers, drained
2 tablespoons chopped Italian parsley

Rinse chicken in cold water and pat dry. Season chicken breasts with salt and pepper. Heat olive oil in a large skillet over medium heat. Add chicken; sauté until cooked through, about 10 minutes. Remove from heat and set aside. In same skillet over medium-low heat, sauté garlic and onion in same oil until softened but not browned. Increase heat to medium, add bell peppers and sauté slowly, stirring often, until softened. Add vinegar and cook, covered, 3 minutes. Add tomatoes and sugar, if necessary, and continue to cook, uncovered, until juices thicken. Season with salt and pepper. Add more olive oil, if desired. Toss in capers and parsley. Transfer pepper mixture to a rimmed platter; place chicken on the top. Serve warm or at room temperature. Makes 4 to 6 servings.

CHICKEN BREASTS IN CHAMPAGNE SAUCE

An excellent way to use leftover champagne, but open a new bottle, if necessary—this dish is that good.

6 chicken breasts halves, boned,
  skinned
Salt and freshly ground white pepper
  to taste
2 cups Champagne
3 tablespoons unsalted butter, softened
3 tablespoons all-purpose flour
1 cup (1/2 pint) whipping cream
Paprika
Fresh watercress sprigs

Rinse chicken with cold water; pat dry. Season chicken with salt and white pepper; place in a single layer in a non-aluminum pan. Cover with Champagne; bring to a simmer over low heat. Simmer until chicken is just cooked through, about 7 minutes, skimming off any foam that rises to the top. Use a slotted spoon to lift chicken to a warm platter. In a small bowl, cream butter and flour into a paste; whisk into the simmering liquid. Cook, whisking, until liquid begins to thicken. Gradually whisk in whipping cream; simmer until thickened, 5 to 10 minutes. Season sauce with salt and pepper; pour over chicken breasts. Dust lightly with paprika, and garnish with watercress sprigs. Makes 6 servings.

TURKEY STRATA WITH BROCCOLI & WHITE CHEDDAR CHEESE

A variation on an old standby, this dish makes breakfast or brunchtime entertaining a breeze. Fresh fruit and bran muffins are all that are needed to round out the menu.

8 firm-textured white bread slices, crusts removed, cut into 1/2-inch cubes
1/4 cup unsalted butter, melted
2 cups cubed cooked turkey
1 bunch broccoli, cut into flowerets, blanched, drained, or 1 (10-oz.) package frozen broccoli flowerets, thawed, drained
3 cups (12 oz.) shredded white Cheddar cheese
4 large eggs
2-1/2 cups half and half or milk
1 teaspoon salt
1 teaspoon dry mustard
1/2 teaspoon red (cayenne) pepper

Butter a 13" x 9" baking dish and set aside. In a medium-size bowl, toss bread cubes with butter; spread half in the baking dish. Top with layers of half the turkey, broccoli and cheese. Repeat with remaining bread cubes, turkey, broccoli and cheese. In a medium-size bowl, whisk the eggs and half and half together with the salt, mustard and cayenne. Pour evenly over the top layer of cheese. Cover with plastic wrap and refrigerate at least 4 hours or overnight. Preheat oven to 350F (175C). Uncover and bake 30 minutes or until mixture is set and top is lightly browned. Makes 6 to 8 servings.

TURKEY HASH

Using a combination of light and dark meat makes for better flavor. Serve this uptown hash for brunch or dinner with toast points or wild rice and fresh seasonal fruit.

2 tablespoons unsalted butter
1 medium-size onion, chopped
1/2 cup chopped red or green bell pepper, or a combination
2 tablespoons all-purpose flour
1/2 cup whipping cream
1 cup Chicken Stock (page 23)
3 cups diced cooked turkey meat
1 large boiling potato, cooked, peeled, diced
2 tablespoons minced parsley
Salt and freshly ground white pepper to taste
Dash of red (cayenne) pepper
1/4 cup fresh bread crumbs
1/4 cup grated Parmesan cheese (optional)

Preheat broiler. Butter a shallow 1-1/2-quart flameproof baking dish and set aside. Melt butter over low heat in a heavy medium-size saucepan. Add onion; sauté until softened but not browned. Add bell pepper; cook 1 minute, then mix in flour. Cook, stirring occasionally, 3 to 4 minutes; remove from heat. In another small saucepan, heat cream and stock together just until bubbles begin to form around edges. Stir into the flour mixture; cook, stirring, until thickened, about 2 minutes. Stir in turkey, potato, parsley; season with salt, pepper and cayenne. Turn mixture into prepared pan; top with bread crumbs and Parmesan cheese, if desired. Place directly under broiler until brown and bubbly, about 2 minutes. Makes 4 to 6 servings.

Note: This entire recipe can be prepared a day in advance and stored, covered, in the refrigerator. Reheat in oven prior to broiling to be sure hash is heated through. This may also be served in individual au gratin dishes.

CHICKEN BREASTS ROCKEFELLER

Save the oysters for another occasion, and enjoy this version of a dish "as rich as Rockeller." And what better accompaniment could there be than carrot coins and small rolls?

6 chicken breast halves, skinned, boned
Salt and freshly ground white pepper to taste
1/4 cup unsalted butter
4 medium-size shallots, coarsely chopped, or 1/4 cup chopped green onions
1 celery stalk, coarsely chopped
4 cups coarsely chopped spinach leaves
1/3 cup fresh bread crumbs
1/4 cup chopped parsley
2 tablespoons Pernod or anisette
Pinch of red (cayenne) pepper
1 large egg
1/4 cup whipping cream
4 bacon slices, crisp-cooked, crumbled

Preheat oven to 350F (175C). Rinse chicken in cold water and pat dry. Butter a 9-inch-square baking pan. Flatten chicken breasts until 1/4 inch thick and season chicken with salt and pepper. Arrange in prepared pan in a single layer and set aside. In a large skillet over medium heat, melt butter. Add shallots and celery; sauté until softened but not browned. Add spinach; sauté about 1 minute or until wilted, then remove pan from heat. Place spinach mixture in a blender or food processor fitted with the steel blade. Add bread crumbs, parsley, Pernod, cayenne, egg and cream; process until smooth. Add salt and pepper to taste. Spread mixture over the top of each breast half, covering completely, and top with bacon. Bake 25 minutes or until chicken is cooked through. Makes 4 to 6 servings.

BREASTS OF CHICKEN FAUX CHAUD-FROID

Stunning enough for a summer luncheon or wedding buffet, its make-ahead feature makes it simple. Serve on a bed of fresh watercress garnished with shiny Niçoise olives.

12 chicken breast halves, poached in
    Chicken Stock (page 23) and
    cooled, skinned and boned
2 (1/4-oz.) envelopes unflavored
    gelatin (2 tablespoons)
1 tablespoon lemon juice
2 cups Basic Mayonnaise (page 141)
1 cup (1/2 pint) dairy sour cream
Salt and freshly ground white pepper
    to taste
Fresh chives
Roasted red bell pepper cutouts (small
    hearts, flowers, etc.)
Fresh tarragon or other herb sprigs
Fresh edible flowers such as
    nasturtiums, borage or chive
    flowers

ASPIC GLAZE:

1 (1/4-oz.) envelope unflavored gelatin
    (1 tablespoon)
2 tablespoons cold water
1-1/2 cups hot water or white wine,
    or a combination

Pat the chicken breasts dry; remove any bits of fat or skin clinging to them. Place a wire rack over a baking sheet or other pan lined with waxed paper to facilitate cleanup later. Soften the gelatin in the lemon juice and set aside. In the top of a double boiler or a heavy medium-size saucepan, combine the Mayonnaise and sour cream; season with salt and pepper. Gently heat until warm, then add the gelatin mixture and stir until gelatin has dissolved completely. Cool to tepid.

Spoon a bit of the mayonnaise mixture over each piece of chicken and let set. Spoon on a second coat and decorate with herbs and edible flowers. Refrigerate at least 30 minutes to set completely. Spoon aspic over coated chicken to glaze. Refrigerate again until set. These can be made a day in advance and stored covered in the refrigerator, taking care that the cover does not touch the aspic. These should be served chilled, but not ice cold. Makes 12 servings.

ASPIC GLAZE:

Combine gelatin with the cold water in a small bowl. Let stand until softened. Stir in hot water until dissolved. Cool until aspic is near the point of jelling, but is still thoroughly liquid.

DUCK BREASTS WITH SPIRITED CRANBERRY SAUCE

I like to serve this attractive entree on a bed of bitter escarole with individual Roquefort Cheese Mousses (page 149). Serve a light first course, such as marinated asparagus, with lots of crusty French bread to eat throughout the meal.

2 duck breasts, boned, halved
1/4 cup sugar
1/4 cup water
1/2 cup raspberry vinegar or other wine vinegar
Salt and freshly ground pepper to taste
1 tablespoon olive oil
2 cups Chicken Stock (page 23)
1-1/2 cups fresh or frozen cranberries, thawed
1/2 cup dry red wine
1 small head of escarole, rinsed, dried
1/4 cup Tawny port or cranberry liqueur
2 tablespoons unsalted butter, softened
1 tablespoon chopped fresh thyme leaves or 1 teaspoon dried leaf thyme

Rinse duck breasts in cold water and pat dry. Heat sugar and water in a small, heavy saucepan over low heat until sugar dissolves, swirling pan occasionally instead of stirring. Increase heat to medium and boil until the sugar caramelizes and is a rich mahogany brown and has a sauce-like consistency. Remove from heat and carefully pour in vinegar (mixture will bubble up) and set aside.

With a sharp knife, score duck skin into crisscross patterns and season well with salt and pepper. Set a large heavy skillet over medium-high heat until very hot. Add oil. Brown duck, skin-side down, in pan until rare, about 7 minutes. Drain all but 1 tablespoon of fat from the pan and quickly sear the second side 1 to 2 minutes. Remove duck from skillet and set aside. Drain fat from skillet and stir in reserved vinegar mixture, scraping up any browned bits clinging to the pan. Add stock, cranberries and red wine and boil until sauce has reduced by half, 10 to 15 minutes.

Meanwhile, preheat broiler. Broil duck breasts, skin-side up, until skin is crisp. Place on a cutting board. Divide escarole among 4 dinner plates and set aside. Slice duck breasts lengthwise into thin, diagonal slices and fan across the escarole. Remove sauce from heat and whisk in port and butter. Add thyme and adjust seasonings to taste. Spoon sauce over the duck breasts, drizzling it lightly over escarole as well. Serve immediately. Makes 4 servings.

SAFFRON FETTUCINE WITH DUCK LIVERS

The stock, pasta and crème fraîche can all be made days in advance. In addition to being delicious, crème fraîche does not break down and separate when heated, as does sour cream. You may want to double the recipe so you'll have this slightly tart cream left over as a cool topping for fresh fruit. This makes a very impressive first course or entree, served with assorted greens tossed in walnut oil.

1 cup Crème Fraîche (recipe below)
4 tablespoons olive oil
4 large shallots, minced
8 wild or cultivated mushrooms, halved
2 tablespoons chopped Italian parsley
1 teaspoon grated lemon zest
1 cup Duck Stock (page 23), or Chicken Stock (page 23)
Salt and freshly ground pepper to taste
12 duck livers
1 pound Saffron Pasta (page 154), cut into strips for fettucine
Italian parsley sprigs (optional)

CRÈME FRAÎCHE:
1 cup (1/2 pint) whipping cream (not ultra-pasteurized)
1 tablespoon buttermilk

Make crème fraîche 1 or 2 days ahead. Heat 2 tablespoons of the olive oil in a large non-aluminum skillet over medium heat. Add shallots and mushrooms; sauté until shallots are softened but not browned. Stir in the chopped parsley and lemon zest, then the stock and crème fraîche and reduce heat to low. Cook until slightly thickened, 5 to 10 minutes. Season with salt and pepper. Meanwhile, in another pan, heat the remaining 2 tablespoons oil. Add livers; sauté over medium-high heat until still slightly pink in the center, 5 to 7 minutes. Cook pasta until *al dente*, 1 or 2 minutes. Drain and toss in the skillet containing the sauce, until pasta is well coated. Place pasta on individual warmed plates and garnish with duck livers and parsley sprigs, if desired. Serve immediately. Makes 4 to 6 servings.

CRÈME FRAÎCHE:
Combine cream and buttermilk in a small heavy saucepan over medium heat. Warm only enough to remove the chill, about 90F (30C) on an instant-reading thermometer. Pour into a clean glass jar, cover loosely and place in a warm place 12 to 24 hours, until the crème fraîche has thickened to the consistency of sour cream. Seal airtight and refrigerate at least 6 hours before using. Store in the refrigerator up to 3 weeks. Makes about 1 cup.

PAN-ROASTED QUAIL WITH HONEY & THYME SAUCE

As is the case with so many favorite recipes for entertaining, advance preparation makes this a very easy and delicious dish to serve to guests.

4 quail (about 6 oz. each), split in
    half, back and small bones
    discarded or saved for stock
Marinade (recipe below)
1 teaspoon salt
1/2 teaspoon freshly ground pepper
1 teaspoon chopped fresh thyme leaves
    or 1/4 teaspoon dried thyme leaves
1/4 cup unsalted butter
1 tablespoon olive oil
Honey & Thyme Sauce (recipe below)

MARINADE:
1/2 cup olive oil
1 teaspoon coarsely cracked
    peppercorns
1 bay leaf
1 garlic clove, crushed
3 thyme sprigs or 1 teaspoon dried
    leaf thyme
3 parsley sprigs

HONEY & THYME SAUCE:
1/4 cup raspberry vinegar or other
    vinegar
2 tablespoons honey
1-1/2 cups Chicken Stock (page 23)
1 teaspoon thyme leaves and flowers
1/2 teaspoon salt
Freshly ground pepper to taste

Rinse quail with cold water and pat dry. Make marinade 24 to 36 hours ahead. Add quail to marinade; cover and refrigerate up to 36 hours, turning 3 or 4 times. Remove quail from marinade and pat dry with paper towels. Season with salt, pepper and thyme. In a large skillet over medium-high heat, melt butter with olive oil. Add quail; sauté 2 to 4 minutes on each side, or until golden. (Sauté in 2 batches, if necessary). Transfer quail to a warm platter and set aside. Reserve skillet to make sauce. Make sauce. Pour sauce over the quail and serve immediately. Makes 4 first-course servings or 2 main-dish servings.

MARINADE:
Combine all ingredients in a large non-aluminum bowl.

HONEY & THYME SAUCE
Discard cooking fat and deglaze skillet with vinegar, scraping up any browned bits which cling to the skillet. Cook over medium-high heat until vinegar has reduced by half. Add honey; when it begins to caramelize, whisk in stock and reduce heat to low. Stir in thyme and simmer about 10 minutes. Add salt and pepper, if needed.

QUAIL WITH WILD RICE & BLACKBERRY SAUCE

Using boned quail makes this dish ideal for a formal dinner party. Quail can be sautéed in advance and finished off in the oven just before serving.

16 boned quail
Salt and freshly ground white pepper
   to taste
4 tablespoons unsalted butter
8 ounces fresh wild or cultivated
   mushrooms, finely chopped
3/4 cup Basic Wild Rice (page 151)
2 tablespoons olive oil
Blackberry Sauce (recipe below)
1/2 cup fresh blackberries, for garnish

Blackberry Sauce:
1/4 cup Chicken Stock (page 23), or
   other poultry stock
1 cup blackberry brandy
8 tablespoons unsalted butter, softened
1-1/2 cups blackberries
Salt and freshly ground pepper to taste

Preheat oven to 400F (205C). Rinse quail with cold water, pat dry and season inside and out with salt and pepper. In a large non-aluminum skillet over medium heat, melt 2 tablespoons of the butter. Add mushrooms; sauté until lightly cooked, about 4 minutes. Toss in wild rice to combine, transfer to a bowl and cool to room temperature. Place a heaping tablespoon of rice mixture inside each quail; tie with string to resemble original shape. In the same skillet over medium heat, melt the remaining 2 tablespoons butter with olive oil. Add quail; quickly sauté until golden-brown on all sides. Discard cooking fat but reserve pan for making sauce. Transfer quail to a baking pan and roast 10 minutes, or until heated through. Make Blackberry Sauce. Blot quail with paper towels and remove string. Keep warm while making sauce. Serve on a heated plate, drizzling sauce over the quail. Garnish each serving with blackberries. Makes 8 servings.

BLACKBERRY SAUCE:

Place the large skillet in which quail were sautéed over medium-high heat and deglaze with stock, scraping up any browned bits which cling to the bottom of the pan. Add brandy and boil until slightly syrupy, about 5 minutes. Reduce heat to low and whisk in butter, 1 tablespoon at a time. Stir in 3/4 of berries, season with salt and pepper, remove from heat and serve immediately.

Accompaniments

$\mathscr{H}$ow that I've cooked it, what do I serve with it? Poultry, with its subtle flavor and silken texture, is a perfect foil for any number of starches.

Once shunned as "fattening," enlightened eaters now recognize the dietary value of carbohydrates. Instead of automatically reaching into the potato bin, vary your mealtime selections with rice, grain and pasta dishes.

Substituting homemade Chicken Stock (page 23) for some or all of the water when cooking grains will add new depths of flavor to these somewhat bland starches. If using canned chicken broth, however, cut down on the amount of salt you add to the cooking liquid.

You can create your own original entree or side dish by mixing compound butters (pages 136 to 137), vegetables, cracklings (page 22) or leftover poultry into cooked rice or pasta.

The creative use of sauces and condiments is another way to turn an everyday dinner into a memorable meal. In addition to the obvious flavor dividends, these little extras add both color and texture to your poultry entree.

Don't get in a rut by serving the same predictable side dishes with every meal. Variety is truly the spice of life so add a little excitement to your family dinner tonight.

Classic Barbecued Chicken, page 106; Bruschetta, page 149

BREADS

BRIOCHE

1/4 cup milk
1 (1/4-oz.) package (1 tablespoon) active dry
  yeast
2-3/4 cups all-purpose flour
4 large eggs
2 tablespoons sugar
1/2 teaspoon salt
1 cup unsalted butter, softened

Heat milk to 110F (45C) and pour into the bowl of a heavy-duty electric mixer. Stir in yeast to dissolve; let stand until foamy, about 5 minutes, then stir in 1/3 cup of flour to form a sticky batter, called a sponge. Pour all the remaining flour over top of this sponge, cover bowl with plastic wrap and a towel, and set aside in a draft-free spot 1 to 2 hours, or until batter begins to bubble up through the flour.

Using the dough hook attachment, mix the sponge and flour at slow speed; add 3 of the eggs, one at a time, then the sugar and salt. Knead until dough is shiny and elastic. (The dough will begin to wrap itself around the dough hook when it is ready.) Add butter, 1 to 2 tablespoons at a time until it is all incorporated. Continue kneading until the dough is shiny and elastic and once again wraps itself around the dough hook. Cover the bowl with plastic wrap and a towel; let rise in a draft-free place 2-1/2 to 3 hours, or until tripled in bulk. Punch down the dough. Grease a large bowl. Add dough to greased bowl. Cover with plastic wrap and refrigerate overnight.

Grease a 9" x 5" loaf pan. Shape dough into a loaf; place in greased pan. Cover loosely with buttered plastic wrap or parchment paper. Let rise until double in bulk. Preheat oven to 350F (175C). Lightly beat remaining egg; brush loaf with beaten egg. Bake 45 minutes, or until golden-brown. Remove from pan and cool on wire rack. (Baked loaf may be frozen.) Makes 1 loaf.

To make by hand: Mix with a wooden spoon. Knead by hand until shiny and elastic, about 10 minutes. Knead in butter 1 to 2 tablespoons at a time. Continue kneading until dough is shiny and elastic.

BUTTERMILK BISCUITS

You'll enjoy these authentic southern biscuits with all kinds of meals.

1-1/2 cups cake flour
1/2 teaspoon salt
1-1/2 teaspoons baking powder
1/4 teaspoon baking soda
3 tablespoons vegetable shortening, chilled
1/2 cup buttermilk, chilled

Preheat oven to 450F (230C). Line a baking sheet with parchment paper. In a medium-size bowl, sift together flour, salt, baking powder and baking soda. Using a pastry blender or two knives, cut in the shortening until mixture resembles coarse meal. Add buttermilk all at once and quickly mix in with a fork. Turn out on a lightly floured board; knead about 30 seconds. Pat dough out to 1/2 inch thick. Cut into 12 (2") rounds with a biscuit cutter. Place on parchment-lined baking sheet. Bake 12 to 15 minutes, or until tops are golden-brown. Makes about 12 biscuits.

STUFFINGS

EVERYONE'S FAVORITE SIDE DISH

Stuffing probably originated as an economical and flavorful way to satisfy ravenous appetites and stretch the number of servings generated from one roasted bird. Stuffing is now as much a part of our holiday traditions as the glistening bird itself, and can still be a thrifty way to use up odds and ends from the refrigerator while creating a fragrant, tasty side dish. Since the major ingredient of so many stuffings is bread, it is important not to skimp on quality. Use firm-textured homemade or store-bought bread, or even some of the commercially made stuffing mixes for ultimate texture and flavor. Bread will be best if cubed or crumbled when fresh, spread out in a single layer on a baking sheet and allowed to dry, uncovered, overnight at room temperature or on top of a turned-off gas burner on the stove. Lacking such foresight, bread can be dried in a 250F (120C) oven 10 to 15 minutes. Corn bread is easiest to crumble after it loses its freshness, so make a pan of it a day or two in advance and leave at room temperature, uncovered, to dry out.

Poultry neck and breast cavities can be loosely filled with stuffing just prior to roasting, or stuffing can be baked in a separate pan. The main problem with stuffing a bird is that in order to cook the stuffing, you usually overcook the meat. Stuffing cooks faster in a separate pan, is less likely to have been contaminated with bacteria and makes for easier and safer storage of leftovers. The cavities of the bird can instead be enhanced with fresh herbs and coarsely sliced aromatic vegetables or fruits, such as celery, onion, oranges or apples that are discarded at serving time. The bird will cook faster and taste just as good as you remember, or even better.

Bake stuffing in a well-buttered casserole, set inside a large pan of hot water at 325F (165C) for 30 to 60 minutes. Baking uncovered in a water bath keeps the interior moist while the top gets crusty. Some cooks like to scatter two or three coarsely chopped pieces of uncooked bacon over the top to add extra moisture and flavor as the stuffing cooks, but using bits of turkey skin, from the neck, will give a more traditional poultry flavor. If not using either of these self-basting techniques, baste the stuffing two or three times with juices from the roasting pan to impart that extra bit of turkey flavor.

Using uncooked eggs in stuffing destined for a bird's cavity is inviting trouble. This creates an ideal environment for bacteria to multiply while you wait for the oven's heat to finally penetrate the breastbone and cook the eggs. For those who prefer stuffing with a lighter, soufflé-like texture, mix in one large uncooked egg for about every four cups of bread used in the stuffing, and bake separately from the bird. The stuffing will take a bit longer to cook, so be sure to check the center for doneness. Here are a few more pointers to make your stuffing truly delicious.

• Allow 3/4 to 1 cup stuffing per pound of turkey.

• If using commercial soft white bread, reduce the liquid in the stuffing recipe to prevent sogginess in the baked stuffing.

• When mixing stuffing, toss lightly with your hands. It is important to keep the mixture light and airy to promote even cooking.

• Never pack stuffing tightly into the bird's cavities. This slows up the heating process, resulting in a longer roasting time that will surely overcook the bird. Also, it is important to allow room for the moisture to expand the bread; tightly packed stuffing becomes gluey and leaden. Leftover stuffing can be baked in a casserole in the oven.

• Stuffing without egg may be prepared as much as a day in advance as long as it is stored in a separate container in the refrigerator. Bring stuffing back to room temperature before stuffing the bird so it will cook at the same rate as the turkey.

- Enrich stuffings with the addition of sautéed chopped poultry livers and hearts.

- For an untrussed turkey, lightly butter an end piece or regular slice of day-old bread to contain the stuffing inside the open cavity.

- Never stuff a bird until just before placing in the oven for roasting. Allowing stuffing to sit in an uncooked bird for even 15 minutes at room temperature creates a health hazard.

- To further reduce the risk of food poisoning, remove all stuffing from the cavity of the bird *immediately* after roasting and place in a serving bowl.

- For a change of pace, loosen the skin over the bird's breast and legs and place stuffing between the skin and the meat (see page 17.)

SAUSAGE & APPLE STUFFING

This versatile stuffing complements light as well as dark poultry.

8 cups cubed French or Italian bread, day old or oven dried
1 pound bulk sausage meat, crumbled
2 tablespoons unsalted butter
1 large onion, chopped
1/2 cup Chicken Stock (page 23)
2 large apples, pared, chopped
1/2 cup raisins
1 teaspoon salt
1 tablespoon chopped fresh sage leaves or 1 teaspoon dried leaf sage

Place bread cubes in a large bowl and set aside. In a medium-size skillet over medium heat, sauté sausage until well browned, about 10 minutes. Transfer sausage to paper towels to drain and discard drippings. In the same skillet, melt butter. Add onion; sauté until softened but not browned. Stir in stock, apples and raisins; bring to a boil. Pour over bread cubes and mix in sausage, salt and sage. Makes about 10 cups.

BREAD STUFFING

This aromatic combination is always a favorite.

1/2 cup unsalted butter
1 cup minced onions
3/4 cup minced celery including some leaves
8 cups of 1/2-inch day-old bread cubes or 8 cups soft bread crumbs
2 teaspoons poultry seasoning
2 teaspoons salt
1/2 teaspoon freshly ground pepper
1/4 cup minced parsley
1/3 cup Chicken Stock (page 23)

In a large skillet over medium heat, melt butter. Add onions and celery; sauté until softened but not browned. Turn into a large bowl, adding remaining ingredients and toss to combine. Makes about 8 cups.

VARIATION

CHESTNUT STUFFING
Prepare as above, using only 6 cups of bread cubes and 1-1/2 teaspoons poultry seasoning. Mix in 1 pound of coarsely chopped cooked chestnuts.

Wild Rice & Mushroom Stuffing

This is a natural for small game birds.

4 ounces bacon
4 ounces fresh mushrooms, minced
1 medium-size onion, minced
1/3 cup chopped celery
1 cup wild rice
1-1/2 teaspoons fresh chopped thyme leaves or
   1/2 teaspoon dried leaf thyme
3 cups Chicken Stock (page 23)
1 teaspoon salt
1/8 teaspoon freshly ground pepper
1/4 cup minced dried apricots (optional)

In a large heavy skillet, sauté bacon until crisp, then remove with tongs or a slotted spoon to paper towels to drain. In the same skillet over medium heat, add mushrooms, onion and celery until softened but not browned. Mince bacon and stir into skillet, along with rice and thyme. Add stock, salt, pepper and apricots, cover and bring to a boil. Uncover and boil gently, without stirring, about 30 minutes until rice is just barely tender. Drain liquid and set, uncovered, over very low heat to dry about 3 minutes, shaking occasionally. Adjust seasonings. Cool before stuffing poultry. Makes about 4 cups.

Bacon & Oyster Stuffing

1/2 cup unsalted butter
1 large onion, finely chopped
1/2 cup chopped celery
3-1/2 cups coarsely crumbled dry bread crumbs
1/4 cup chopped parsley
1 quart raw oysters, coarsely chopped
1/2 cup oyster liquor
4 ounces bacon, crisp-cooked, coarsely crumbled
Salt and freshly ground pepper to taste
1 tablespoon chopped fresh thyme leaves or 1
   teaspoon dried leaf thyme

In a large skillet, melt butter. Add onion and celery; sauté until softened but not browned. Remove from heat, add bread crumbs and parsley and mix thoroughly. Add oysters, oyster liquor, bacon, salt, pepper and thyme. Makes about 10 cups.

Kentucky Corn Bread & Pecan Stuffing

You'll find a lot of pleasant surprises in this tasty stuffing.

4 cups dried or day-old crumbled corn bread
2/3 cup coarsely chopped pecans, toasted
8 ounces pancetta
3/4 cup unsalted butter
2 celery stalks, chopped
2 onions, chopped
1 tablespoon chopped fresh thyme leaves or 1
   teaspoon dried leaf thyme
1 tablespoon chopped fresh sage leaves or 1
   teaspoon dried leaf sage
Salt and freshly ground pepper to taste
1/2 cup whipping cream
2/3 cup Poultry Stock (page 23)
1/4 cup bourbon

Place corn bread and pecans in a large bowl and set aside. In a large non-aluminum skillet over medium heat, sauté the pancetta in 2 tablespoons of the butter until slightly crisp. Add to corn bread. Melt remaining 4 tablespoons butter in same skillet. Add celery and onions; sauté until softened but not browned. Stir in thyme, sage, salt and pepper, then add to corn bread. Add cream, stock and bourbon to the skillet, stirring and scraping with a wooden spoon to loosen any browned bits in the skillet. Bring to a boil; cook 10 minutes. Add to corn bread mixture. Toss well and adjust seasonings. Cool mixture before stuffing bird. Makes about 7-1/2 cups.

Compound Butters, Sauces & Chutneys

Compound Butters

These colorful butters all start with the same basic ingredient: unsalted butter is softened and combined with other flavors, formed into a 1-inch-diameter log and refrigerated until firm enough to slice. They can be frozen for up to two months so you can always have a savory pick-me-up on hand for plain, grilled or roasted fowl, vegetables, pasta or breads.

Southwestern Butter

1 cup unsalted butter, softened
3 tablespoons minced cilantro
3 tablespoons minced parsley
1/2 teaspoon ground cumin
1 small jalapeño pepper, minced, with some seeds
1 small red chile pepper, minced, with some seeds
1 garlic clove, minced
1/4 teaspoon salt

Combine all ingredients in a food processor fitted with the metal blade; process until combined. Or mix with a wooden spoon in a small bowl. Form into 1 or 2 logs on plastic wrap and roll up, twisting ends to seal. Refrigerate or freeze. Makes about 2 cups.

Basil Butter

1 cup unsalted butter, softened
1/2 cup tightly packed basil leaves
2 garlic cloves, minced
1 tablespoon fresh lemon juice, or to taste

Prepare as for Southwestern Butter. Makes about 2 cups.

Lemon Caper Butter

1 cup unsalted butter, softened
3 tablespoons fresh lemon juice
1/2 teaspoon grated lemon zest
1 tablespoon Dijon-style mustard
1 tablespoon capers, drained

Prepare as for Southwestern Butter. Makes about 2 cups.

Herb Butter

1 cup unsalted butter, softened
3 tablespoons finely chopped chives
2 tablespoons finely chopped parsley
1 tablespoon chopped fresh herbs of choice such as tarragon, dill, sage
1 small garlic clove, minced (optional)
1/4 teaspoon fresh lemon juice

Prepare as for Southwestern Butter. Makes about 2 cups.

Sun-dried Tomato Butter

1 cup unsalted butter, softened
1 small garlic clove, minced
1/4 to 1/3 cup oil-packed sun-dried tomatoes, drained, minced

Prepare as for Southwestern Butter. Makes about 2 cups.

Roquefort Butter

3/4 cup unsalted butter, softened
2 ounces Roquefort Cheese, or to taste
Dash of red (cayenne) pepper
1 tablespoon minced fresh parsley

Prepare as for Southwestern Butter. Makes about 2 cups.

NUTTY CRANBERRY BUTTER

2 cups fresh cranberries, rinsed, picked over,
   coarsely chopped
1/2 cup fresh orange juice
1/2 cup packed light-brown sugar
Zest of 1 orange, minced
3/4 cup unsalted butter, softened
1/2 cup finely chopped toasted pecans

Prepare as for Southwestern Butter. Makes about
2 cups.

HONEY OR MAPLE BUTTER

1 cup unsalted butter, softened
1/2 to 2/3 cup honey or maple syrup, to taste

Prepare as for Southwestern Butter. Makes about
2 cups.

CHUTNEY BUTTER

1 cup unsalted butter, softened
1/2 cup Nectarine Chutney (page 116) or bottled
   chutney
2 teaspoons curry powder (optional)

Prepare as for Southwestern Butter. Makes about
2 cups.

TARRAGON BUTTER

2 shallots, minced
1/4 cup tarragon vinegar
1 cup unsalted butter, softened
1/3 cup minced tarragon leaves

In a small, non-aluminum saucepan, boil shallots
in the vinegar until only a teaspoon of liquid
remains in the pan. Remove from heat and cool 5
to 10 minutes. Combine shallot mixture with
butter and tarragon in a food processor fitted with
the metal blade; process until combined. Or mix
with a wooden spoon in a small bowl. Form into 1
or 2 logs on plastic wrap and roll up, twisting ends
to seal. Refrigerate or freeze. Makes about 2 cups.

RED PEPPER BUTTER

2 tablespoons unsalted butter
4 shallots, minced
4 medium-size red bell peppers, peeled, seeded
   and minced
2 tablespoons balsamic vinegar
1 cup unsalted butter, softened

In a small skillet, melt the 2 tablespoons of butter. Add shallots, bell pepper and vinegar; cook
just until softened. Cool slightly. Combine softened butter and bell pepper mixture in a food
processor fitted with the metal blade; process
until combined. Or mix with a wooden spoon in
a small bowl. Form into 1 or 2 logs on plastic wrap
and roll up, twisting ends to seal. Refrigerate or
freeze. Makes about 2 cups.

SAUCE VELOUTÉ

This classic French sauce is a natural with any poultry.

2 tablespoons unsalted butter
2 tablespoons all-purpose flour
2 cups Chicken Stock (page 23), heated
Kosher salt and freshly ground white pepper to
    taste

In a medium-size saucepan, melt butter over low heat. Whisk in flour and cook, stirring, 2 or 3 minutes to eliminate raw taste of flour. Pour stock slowly into the flour mixture, whisking constantly. Reduce heat; simmer over low heat 25 to 30 minutes to thicken sauce. Season with salt and pepper and strain through a fine sieve before serving. Makes about 1-1/4 cups.

VARIATIONS

VELOUTÉ MORNAY
Mix 1 cup shredded cheese, such as Swiss, Cheddar or Parmesan, and 1/2 cup dry white wine into strained Sauce Velouté. Makes about 2 cups.

MUSTARD VELOUTÉ
Mix 2 teaspoons Dijon-style mustard into strained Sauce Velouté. Makes about 1-1/4 cups.

SOUBISE VELOUTÉ
In a small skillet over medium heat, sauté 2 large onions in 1/4 cup butter until softened but not browned. Add 3 tablespoons dry white wine and cook 2 to 3 minutes to reduce. Puree mixture in a food processor or blender and add to strained Sauce Velouté. Makes about 2 cups.

FRESH TOMATO SAUCE

Use this sauce for everything from pizza to polenta.

1 tablespoon olive oil
1 onion, coarsely chopped
8 medium-size tomatoes, seeded, coarsely chopped
1 garlic clove, minced
1 tablespoon chopped parsley
1 tablespoon fresh thyme leaves or 1 teaspoon
    dried leaf thyme
Kosher salt and freshly ground pepper to taste

Heat oil in a large non-aluminum skillet. Add onion; sauté until softened but not browned. Add tomatoes, garlic, parsley, thyme, salt and pepper. Simmer gently until mixture has been reduced to a thick pulp, about 30 minutes. Strain sauce through a fine sieve. For a thicker sauce, return to skillet and reduce to desired consistency over medium heat. Makes about 1 cup.

VARIATIONS

TOMATO CREAM SAUCE
Add 1/2 cup warm whipping cream to strained sauce.
Substitute basil or oregano for the thyme.

TIP

To prevent a skin from forming on a sauce as it cools, place a piece of plastic wrap directly on the surface.

CREAMY MUSHROOM SAUCE

Some fresh thyme leaves or a bit of wine substituted for part of the liquid would give added dimension to this sauce.

3 tablespoons unsalted butter
1/2 pound fresh mushrooms, sliced
1 tablespoon all-purpose flour
1 teaspoon soy sauce
3/4 cup half and half or 1/2 cup half and half and 1/4 cup Chicken Stock (page 23)
Salt and freshly ground pepper to taste

Melt butter in a large skillet over medium heat. Add mushrooms, sprinkle with flour and cook, stirring occasionally, 8 to 10 minutes. Add soy sauce, then slowly stir in the half and half. Cook, stirring occasionally, until the mixture has thickened enough to lightly coat the back of a spoon. Season with salt and pepper. Makes about 1-1/2 cups.

CHICKEN AU JUS

This low-calorie French-style gravy enhances the flavor of roast chicken. Double this recipe for larger birds.

1 (3-1/2-lb.) chicken, roasted
1-1/4 cups Chicken Stock (page 23)
Dash of dry white wine or lemon juice
Salt and pepper to taste

Remove chicken to a warm serving platter to rest and pour out as much fat from the roasting pan as possible. Place pan over medium heat on top of the stove, stirring and scraping with a wooden spoon to loosen any browned bits which cling to the pan. Add stock and wine and bring to a boil, stirring occasionally, until reduced by almost half. Season and strain, if desired. Makes about 1/2 cup.

PAN GRAVY

If you prefer a perfectly smooth gravy, strain through a fine sieve before serving. Double this recipe for a large turkey.

Roasted poultry
2 cups Chicken Stock (page 23)
1/4 cup unsalted butter
1/4 cup all-purpose flour
Salt and freshly ground pepper to taste

Remove roasted bird to a warm serving platter to rest and pour out as much fat from the roasting pan as possible. Pour stock into pan and stir and scrape with a wooden spoon to loosen any browned bits which cling to the pan. In a heavy bottomed 1-1/2-quart saucepan over medium heat, melt butter and whisk in flour. Cook, stirring occasionally, 1 or 2 minutes, or until flour has just turned golden. Add stock and pan drippings and whisk until thickened. Season with salt and pepper. Makes about 2 cups.

VARIATIONS

CREAM GRAVY
Prepare as directed above using 1-1/2 cups stock and 1/2 cup half and half for liquid.

MILK GRAVY
Prepare as directed above using 1 cup each of stock and whole milk for liquid.

HERB GRAVY
Prepare as directed above, adding 1 tablespoon of chopped fresh herbs such as thyme or sage.

GIBLET GRAVY
Prepare as directed using Giblet Stock (page 23), adding water, wine, or chicken stock to giblet stock to equal 2 cups, if necessary. Mix in minced cooked giblets and neck meat just before serving.

Basic Mayonnaise

A well seasoned homemade mayonnaise bears little resemblance to the commercial condiment most of us were raised on. Mayonnaise is a close relative to the other famous emulsion sauces, hollandaise and béarnaise, in that it is a combination of eggs and fat bound together with acid.

Making your own mayonnaise assures you of a preservative-free product made with the freshest ingredients available, and puts you in control of the amount of salt and other flavorings added. The use of polyunsaturated oils makes the cholesterol content of a tablespoon of mayonnaise quite low. Use plain or flavored mayonnaise as a condiment for poached or grilled poultry, in salads, or in sandwiches. Homemade mayonnaise should be stored airtight in the refrigerator and will keep for 7 to 10 days.

1 large egg, at room temperature
1 tablespoon lemon juice or wine vinegar
1 teaspoon kosher salt
1/4 teaspoon freshly ground white pepper
1-1/2 cups vegetable oil

In a food processor fitted with the metal blade, place the egg, lemon juice, salt and pepper. Process until blended, 2 to 3 seconds. With the motor running, pour the oil through the feed tube in a slow, steady stream. When thick, remove from processor and refrigerate. Makes about 1-3/4 cups.

Variations

Pesto Mayonnaise

1 recipe Basic Mayonnaise
2 tablespoons Basic Pesto (page 142), or to taste

Mix herbs with mayonnaise; cover and refrigerate until chilled. Makes about 1-3/4 cups.

Aioli

4 to 6 garlic cloves, minced or crushed
1 recipe Basic Mayonnaise

Mix well with mayonnaise, cover and refrigerate until chilled. Makes about 1-3/4 cups.

Chicken Kabobs with Red Pepper Mayonnaise, page 94

Red Pepper Mayonnaise

3 tablespoons oil
2 shallots, minced
3 large red bell peppers, peeled, seeded, chopped
1 recipe Basic Mayonnaise

Heat oil in a medium-size skillet. Add shallots and peppers; cook until softened but not browned. In a food processor fitted with the metal blade, puree shallots and peppers. Mix well with mayonnaise, cover and refrigerate until chilled. Makes about 2 cups.

Herb Mayonnaise

1/3 cup chopped fresh herbs such as parsley, chives, tarragon, basil, thyme or dill
1 recipe Basic Mayonnaise

Mix herbs with mayonnaise, cover and refrigerate until chilled. Makes about 1-3/4 cups.

Dijon Mayonnaise

1 recipe Basic Mayonnaise
2 or 3 tablespoons Dijon-style mustard

Mix mayonnaise and mustard, cover and refrigerate until chilled. Makes about 1-3/4 cups.

Asian-style Mayonnaise

1 recipe Basic Mayonnaise
1 tablespoon rice wine vinegar
1 walnut-size piece of gingerroot, peeled, minced
1 garlic clove, minced
1 tablespoon light soy sauce
1/2 teaspoon sugar
2 teaspoons sesame oil
2 drops of hot chile oil, or to taste

Make Basic Mayonnaise, substituting rice wine vinegar for lemon or other vinegar. Add remaining ingredients. Mix well, cover and refrigerate until chilled. Makes about 1-3/4 cups.

Chile Mayonnaise

1 teaspoon chili powder or to taste
1 teaspoon ground cumin
1 jalapeño pepper, seeded, minced
1 recipe Basic Mayonnaise

Mix well, cover and refrigerate until chilled. Makes about 1-3/4 cups.

BASIC PESTO

Pesto is a highly aromatic, uncooked sauce traditionally ground with a mortar and pestle. Pesto alla Genovese is the original version, but now there are many variations we can whip up in our blenders or food processors. The final product should be a somewhat grainy paste not a smooth puree.

2 cups lightly packed basil leaves
3 garlic cloves, minced
1/2 cup freshly grated Parmesan cheese
1 tablespoon pine nuts
3/4 cup olive oil
2 teaspoons salt, or freshly ground pepper to taste

In a blender or food processor fitted with the metal blade, puree basil, garlic, cheese, pine nuts, oil and salt. Taste for seasoning and add more salt and pepper, if necessary. Use immediately, or cover and store in refrigerator up to 4 days, or freeze. Makes about 1-1/4 cups.

VARIATIONS

CILANTRO PESTO

2 cups cilantro leaves (about 3 large bunches, or 1/2 lb. *total*)
1/2 bunch Italian parsley
1 large garlic clove, crushed
1/2 cup freshly grated Parmesan cheese
1/3 cup hulled pumpkin seeds (pepitas) or pine nuts
1 tablespoon fresh lime juice or lemon juice
1/4 cup olive oil
Salt and freshly ground pepper to taste

Prepare as for Basic Pesto. Makes about 1-1/4 cups.

ROSEMARY-ORANGE PESTO

2 garlic cloves, crushed
2 tablespoons fresh rosemary leaves
1/2 cup Italian parsley leaves
1 tablespoon grated orange zest
1 cup green onions, coarsely chopped
1/4 teaspoon red (cayenne) pepper
1/2 cup olive oil
2 tablespoons freshly grated Parmesan cheese
1 tablespoon balsamic vinegar
1/4 cup coarsely chopped walnuts, toasted

Prepare as for Basic Pesto. Makes about 1-1/4 cups.

RIPE OLIVE PESTO

2 garlic cloves, crushed
1 tablespoon freshly grated Parmesan cheese
1 (7-oz.) jar Niçoise olives, drained and pitted or 1 cup Kalamata or other oil-cured olives, pitted
1 tablespoon capers, drained
1/2 cup Italian parsley leaves
1/2 cup olive oil
Red (cayenne) pepper and freshly ground black pepper to taste
1 to 2 tablespoons fresh lemon juice
1-1/2 teaspoons chopped fresh thyme leaves or 1/2 teaspoon dried leaf thyme

Prepare as for Basic Pesto. Makes about 1-1/4 cups.

DILL WEED PESTO

1/4 cup walnuts or pine nuts, lightly toasted
2 to 3 garlic cloves, minced
2-1/2 cups dill weed, coarsely chopped (without stems)
3/4 cup olive oil
1/2 teaspoon salt
1/2 teaspoon freshly ground pepper

Prepare as for Basic Pesto. Makes about 1-1/4 cups.

BASIC CRANBERRY SAUCE

Don't reserve this wonderful condiment exclusively for the holidays. Keep cranberries in the freezer so you can enjoy them year around with all types of poultry.

1 cup sugar
3/4 cup water
2 cups fresh or frozen cranberries, rinsed, picked over
1 teaspoon finely grated orange zest (optional)

Combine sugar and water in a medium-size, non-aluminum saucepan over medium heat. Bring to a boil, add cranberries and return to a boil. Reduce heat to medium-low and boil gently 5 to 10 minutes, stirring occasionally until berries just begin to pop. Remove from heat and stir in orange zest, if desired. Cool to room temperature and store, covered, in refrigerator. Serve, chilled or at room temperature, within 4 days. Makes about 2 cups.

VARIATION

SPICED CRANBERRY SAUCE
Place 6 whole cloves, 6 whole allspice and 1 cinnamon stick in a cheesecloth square and tie with kitchen string. Add along with cranberries and remove before serving.

CRANBERRY SALSA

Try this for a snappy break from tradition!

1-1/2 cups fresh or frozen cranberries, rinsed, picked over
2 green onions, minced
1 small jalapeño pepper, minced
1/3 cup sugar
3 tablespoons minced cilantro
3 tablespoons fresh lime juice

Coarsely slice or chop cranberries by hand or in a food processor. Place cranberries in a small glass or ceramic bowl and toss well with the onions, pepper, sugar, cilantro and lime. Cover and refrigerate overnight to allow flavors to blend. Serve, chilled or at room temperature, within 4 days. Makes 1 cup.

CRANBERRY HORSERADISH RELISH

A tart and zesty undercurrent balances the sweetness of the berries.

4 cups fresh or frozen cranberries, rinsed, picked over
3/4 cup sugar
2 tablespoons raspberry vinegar or other vinegar
1 tablespoon drained prepared horseradish

Coarsely chop cranberries by hand or in a food processor. Transfer to a bowl and toss well with sugar, vinegar and horseradish. Cover and refrigerate at least 1 hour to allow flavors to blend. Serve, chilled or at room temperature within 4 days. Makes about 2-1/2 cups.

TIP

It's not necessary to thaw frozen cranberries before adding them to a recipe.

CRANBERRY CHUTNEY

3 cups fresh cranberries, rinsed, picked over
2 tart apples, chopped
1-1/2 cups packed dark-brown sugar
1/2 cup raisins, currants or sultanas
2 shallots, chopped
1 teaspoon grated fresh gingerroot
1/2 teaspoon ground curry powder
1/4 teaspoon ground cloves
1/4 teaspoon ground allspice
Zest of 1 orange, chopped
1/4 cup cider vinegar
4 ounces chopped almonds, toasted

In a large, non-aluminum saucepan, bring all ingredients except nuts to a boil. Cook until thickened, stirring occasionally, about 10 minutes. Remove from heat and stir in nuts. Cool. Serve at room temperature. Makes about 4 cups.

CUMBERLAND SAUCE

This classic sauce of British origin is especially tasty with game birds.

2 large shallots, minced
1/3 cup red currant jelly
1/3 cup orange juice
1/3 cup Tawny port
3 tablespoons lemon juice
2 teaspoons cornstarch
1 tablespoon cold water

In a small non-aluminum saucepan over low heat, combine shallots, jelly, orange juice and port. Simmer 10 minutes, then add lemon juice. In a small bowl, dissolve cornstarch in water, then whisk mixture into hot sauce until thickened. Remove from heat, cool to room temperature, cover and refrigerate until serving. Serve chilled. Makes about 1 cup.

GINGERED CRANBERRY SAUCE

This sweet-tart relish is irresistible with all matter of fowl.

4 cups fresh or frozen cranberries, rinsed, picked over
1-1/4 cups sugar
1/2 cup chopped candied stem ginger in syrup (available in Asian markets)
2 tablespoons syrup from the candied ginger
1/4 cup lemon juice or orange juice
2 teaspoons finely grated lemon or orange zest
1/2 cup walnuts, toasted

In a large saucepan, mix cranberries, sugar, ginger, syrup, lemon juice and zest. Bring to a boil over high heat. Reduce heat to low and simmer 5 to 10 minutes, until berries just begin to pop. Remove from heat and stir in walnuts. Cool to room temperature, cover and store in refrigerator. Makes about 3 cups. Serve, chilled or at room temperature, within 4 days.

TIP

Hollowed out citrus shells make ideal containers for condiments such as cranberry sauce.

Glazes, Marinades & Bastes

Poultry Glazes

To create a picture perfect, glistening brown bird, brush periodically with one of the following glazes during the last 20 to 30 minutes of roasting or broiling. You'll need about 1/2 cup glaze for a chicken, 1 to 1-1/2 cups for a turkey and about 1/4 cup for a quail. Leftover glaze can be stored in the refrigerator.

Orange-Honey Glaze

1 (6-oz.) can frozen orange juice concentrate, thawed
3/4 cup honey
1 tablespoon soy sauce

Mix all ingredients in a small saucepan. Stir over low heat until well combined. Makes about 1-1/4 cups.

Variations

Currant Jelly Glaze
1 cup currant jelly
2 tablespoons red wine
2 tablespoons Dijon-style mustard

Prepare as for Orange-Honey Glaze.

Apricot Glaze
1 cup apricot jam
2 tablespoons Amaretto liqueur or brandy

Prepare as for Orange-Honey Glaze.

Cranberry Ginger Glaze
1 cup jellied cranberry sauce
2 tablespoons Port wine
1 tablespoon minced gingerroot

Prepare as for Orange-Honey Glaze.

Spicy Curry Glaze
1 cup red pepper jelly
2 tablespoons fresh lemon juice
1 tablespoon curry powder

Prepare as for Orange-Honey Glaze.

Teriyaki Glaze

Although teriyaki has come to represent any soy-based marinade, teri means "to shine" and yaki means "to sear with heat." True teriyaki foods are first grilled or broiled, then glazed to seal in juices.

1/3 cup soy sauce
1/3 cup sherry
1 tablespoon minced gingerroot
1 tablespoon brown sugar
2 garlic cloves, minced
1 tablespoon sesame oil
3 tablespoons peanut oil

Mix all ingredients together in a small bowl. Makes about 1-1/4 cups.

Tip

Many of these glazes and marinades are also delicious with other meats such as pork roasts or chops.

Marinades & Bastes

Marinades and basting sauces usually contain the same basic components: some sort of fat or oil to provide moisture; an acid such as lemon juice, wine or vinegar to break down the muscle fibers and spices or herbs for flavoring.

Marinating is a leisurely way of flavoring and tenderizing poultry. It is an ideal prelude to broiling and barbecuing, but is also often employed with roasting.

Basting imparts surface flavor to poultry without the advantage of tenderizing, since the acid in the sauce does not have sufficient time to act on the meat's fiber. Since most bastes contain ingredients high in sugar which caramelize with heat, it is important to apply them only during the last 15 minutes of broiling or grilling or the final 30 minutes of roasting to avoid burning.

• If using a frozen bird, be sure to thaw it thoroughly (page 11) and pat dry so as not to dilute the marinade.

• Marinate poultry in a non-aluminum container or a large plastic bag set inside a pan. Turn the bird occasionally to distribute the marinade evenly.

• Unless otherwise directed, marinate up to 2 hours at cool room temperature, or as long as 48 hours in the refrigerator.

• Drain off marinade before cooking, using the extra marinade for basting.

South Seas Marinade

Everyone loves this sweet and spicy marinade.

1/4 cup vegetable oil
1/4 cup soy sauce
1/4 cup fresh pineapple juice
1/4 cup packed light-brown sugar
3 tablespoons sherry
1 tablespoon chopped gingerroot

Mix all ingredients together in a medium-size bowl. To use, add poultry and marinate in the refrigerator 4 hours or overnight. Makes about 1-1/4 cups.

Curry Marinade

This combination of exotic flavors guarantees a memorable meal.

1/2 cup olive oil
1/3 cup fresh lemon juice
1/4 cup curry powder
2 garlic cloves, minced
Dash *each* of red (cayenne) pepper and cumin powder
Pinch of saffron (optional)

Mix all ingredients together in a medium-size bowl. To use, add poultry and marinate in the refrigerator 4 hours or overnight. Makes about 1 cup.

Herbed Orange Marinade

The clean, subtle flavors of citrus and herbs make this a hit.

2/3 cup dry white wine
3 tablespoons olive oil
1/3 cup fresh orange juice
2 tablespoons chopped fresh herbs such as thyme, tarragon or sage, or 1 teaspoon dried leaf herbs
1 garlic clove, minced
Salt and pepper to taste

Mix all ingredients together in a medium-size bowl. To use, add poultry and marinate in refrigerator 4 hours or overnight. Makes about 1 cup.

Tip

Tie branches of herbs, such as rosemary or marjoram, together with a piece of twine and use as a brush to baste poultry.

DIJON MARINADE

This incomparable French-style mustard lends both body and flavor to this marinade.

3 tablespoons red wine vinegar or white wine vinegar
2 tablespoons Dijon-style mustard
1 large shallot, minced
1 teaspoon salt
1 teaspoon freshly ground black pepper
3/4 cup olive oil

Mix all ingredients together in a medium-size bowl. To use, add poultry and marinate in refrigerator 4 hours or overnight. Makes about 1 cup.

BARBECUE SAUCE I

Every American outdoor cook has his or her own concept of the perfect barbecue sauce. To recommend one over another could possibly incite a riot, so here are some favorites listed merely by number —you'll have to make your own decision as to which is best.

Use them as a "mop sauce" for basting, or as a condiment for eating along with poultry. If leftover poultry seems dry, simmer it in your favorite barbecue sauce. These sauces can be kept at least one week in the refrigerator.

1/4 cup olive oil
1 large onion, coarsely chopped
4 garlic cloves, minced
1 (28-oz.) can chopped or pureed tomatoes
1/3 cup packed dark-brown sugar
1/3 cup cider vinegar
1 teaspoon salt
Freshly ground black pepper to taste
Red (cayenne) pepper to taste

Heat oil in a medium-size non-aluminum saucepan over medium heat. Add onion and garlic; sauté, stirring frequently, until softened but not browned, 7 to 10 minutes. Stir in tomatoes, brown sugar, vinegar, salt, black pepper and cayenne. Reduce heat to low and simmer, uncovered, until sauce is reduced to about 2-1/2 cups, about 45 minutes. Makes 2-1/2 cups.

BARBECUE SAUCE II

1-1/2 cups strong black coffee
1 cup ketchup
1/2 cup cider vinegar
1/4 cup Worcestershire sauce
1/4 cup unsalted butter
3 celery stalks, finely chopped
1 small onion, finely chopped
1 teaspoon light-brown sugar
1 teaspoon chili powder
1 teaspoon paprika
2 garlic cloves, minced
2 bay leaves
1/2 teaspoon salt
1/2 teaspoon freshly ground pepper

Combine all ingredients in a medium-size non-aluminum saucepan over medium heat. Bring to a boil, then reduce heat to low and simmer 15 minutes. Remove from heat and discard bay leaves. Makes about 2-1/2 cups.

BARBECUE SAUCE III

2 teaspoons whole cloves
1 (3-inch) cinnamon stick, broken
1 teaspoon celery seeds
1/2 cup fresh lemon juice
1 medium-size onion, minced
1 garlic clove, minced
2 teaspoons salt
3 tablespoons sugar
1/4 teaspoon hot-pepper sauce
1 teaspoon chili powder
2 teaspoons dry mustard
1 (8-oz.) can tomato sauce
1/4 cup olive oil

Tie cloves, cinnamon and celery seeds in a small piece of cheesecloth and place in a small non-aluminum saucepan with lemon juice. Cover and cook over medium heat until mixture boils. Remove from heat and steep, covered, 1 hour. Discard spices and add remaining ingredients. Simmer, uncovered, 15 minutes. Makes about 1-1/2 cups.

Side Dishes

Make-ahead Mashed Potatoes

Advance preparation makes these rich and creamy potatoes ideal for potlucks or buffet-style entertaining. Your local cheese shop or deli should carry natural cream cheese, which is made without additives or gum stabilizers.

8 to 10 medium-sized russet potatoes (about 3-1/2 lbs. *total)*
8 ounces cream cheese (preferably natural cream cheese), at room temperature
1/4 cup dairy sour cream
Salt and white pepper to taste
2 tablespoons unsalted butter, softened
Paprika and/or freshly chopped chives

Butter a 2-quart ovenproof dish. Peel potatoes. Cut in cubes. Cook in salted water until tender in a large saucepan. Drain potatoes. Using an electric mixer at medium speed, beat cream cheese and sour cream until blended. Gradually add hot potatoes, beating until light and fluffy. Season to taste with salt and pepper. Spoon the whipped potatoes into prepared dish and brush surface with softened butter. Cover and refrigerate until needed, or as long as overnight. Preheat oven to 350F (175C). Bake potatoes 30 minutes or until heated through. Sprinkle lightly with paprika and/or chives before serving. Makes 8 servings.

Wild Mushroom Ragout

Delicious with grilled or roasted poultry, mushroom ragout can be made ahead and reheated.

8 medium-size shallots, thinly sliced
2-1/2 to 3 cups julienned or sliced wild mushrooms (such as porcini, shiitake, morels, chanterelles, etc.)
3/4 cup whipping cream
Salt and pepper to taste
1 tablespoon chopped fresh thyme leaves or 1 teaspoon dried leaf thyme
2 teaspoons fresh lemon juice

Combine shallots, mushrooms and cream in a medium-size saucepan over medium-high heat. Bring to a boil, then reduce heat and cook until cream has thickened, 5 to 10 minutes. Season with thyme, salt, pepper and lemon juice. Makes 8 servings.

Parmesan Crisps

Serve these tasty morsels with salads or as a snack with cocktails.

1 (about 1-lb.) package thin won-ton skins
Unsalted butter, melted
Freshly grated Parmesan cheese

Preheat oven to 350F (175C). Cut won-ton skins in half diagonally to make triangular chips. Line a baking sheet with parchment paper or foil and spread skins in a single layer so edges are not touching. Brush with melted butter and sprinkle generously with cheese. Bake 6 to 8 minutes, or until lightly golden. Cool completely. Serve immediately or store airtight. Makes about 140 crisps.

BRUSCHETTA

This rustic garlic bread is enjoyed by the inhabitants of all the countries bordering the Mediterranean. Be sure to make plenty—it's always a hit. It can be grilled along with other food or toasted in the oven.

3/4 cup olive oil
6 medium-size garlic cloves, minced
12 (1-inch-thick) slices of day-old sourdough or
 country-style bread

In a small pan over low heat, heat oil until just warm. Add garlic and remove from heat. Set aside. (Covered tightly, this can be refrigerated several days.) Preheat broiler. Under broiler toast both sides of the bread until golden-brown. Generously brush 1 side of each slice with garlic oil and serve warm. Makes 12 slices.

GRILLED PESTO EGGPLANT

Pesto can be purchased frozen, or made at home when fresh basil is plentiful in the summer.

6 Japanese eggplants, cut in half lengthwise
1/3 cup Basic Pesto, (page 142), or other pesto to
 taste
2 tablespoons olive oil

Preheat gas grill or ignite charcoal and burn until flame is gone and charcoal is covered with a uniform gray ash. Using a small sharp knife, score a uniform crisscross pattern 1/4 to 1/2 inch deep in the flesh of each eggplant half, taking care not to break through the skin. With a small spoon, force the pesto into the cuts, so that the pattern is visible. Lightly brush both sides of eggplants with oil. Grill until flesh is cooked through, about 5 minutes. Makes 6 servings.

ROQUEFORT CHEESE MOUSSE

Make these the day before your dinner party.

1-1/2 teaspoons unflavored gelatin powder
2 tablespoons cold water
3 large egg yolks
3 tablespoons whipping cream
6 ounces Roquefort cheese, pureed in a food
 processor or blender or forced through a sieve
Dash of red (cayenne) pepper
Salt to taste
3/4 cup whipping cream, chilled
2 large egg whites, room temperature
Dash of cream of tartar
1/4 cup finely chopped toasted walnuts

In a small heatproof bowl, combine gelatin and water. Let stand until softened. Place bowl in a pan of simmering water until gelatin has dissolved. Set aside. In a heavy small saucepan set over low heat, whisk egg yolks and 3 tablespoons cream until warm and smooth. Stir in gelatin and cheese. Season with cayenne and salt, if needed. When cheese is completely melted, remove from heat and set aside. In a large bowl, whip the 3/4 cup of cream until stiff peaks form and set aside. In a medium-size bowl, whip egg whites with cream of tartar until stiff peaks form. Fold in about 1/3 of the whipped cream until it is completely incorporated, then fold the entire egg white mixture into the remaining whipped cream. Fold about 1/3 of the whipped mixture into the cheese base to lighten it, then return the cheese mixture to the remaining whipped mixture and fold until completely incorporated. Turn the mixture into 4 (8-oz.) soufflé dishes or ramekins. Refrigerate at least 2 hours or overnight. Garnish with walnuts before serving. Makes 4 servings.

Grains & Pasta

Basic Steamed Rice

Use this chart to make the amount of cooked rice that you need.

Type of Rice	Amount	Stock or water	Butter	Salt	Minutes cooking time	Yield of cooked rice
White (long/short grain)	1 cup	2 cups	1 T.	1 t.	18	3 cups
White (converted type)	1 cup	2-1/2 cups	1 T.	1 t.	20	4 cups
Brown (long grain)	1 cup	2-1/2 cups	1 T.	1 t.	40*	4 cups

Use a heavy pan large enough for the raw rice to triple or quadruple in volume. Add the butter and salt to the cooking liquid; bring to a boil over medium heat. Slowly add the rice. Bring back to a boil, cover pan and reduce heat to low. Simmer, without stirring, for the time listed above. Remove cooked rice from heat and let stand, covered, 5 minutes. Fluff with a fork to separate grains of rice before serving.

*or as directed on package label

Variations

Apricot-Raisin Rice
Add minced dried apricots, coarsely chopped pistachio or pine nuts and dark or golden raisins to cooked rice.

Cheese
Add 1/2 to 3/4 cup freshly grated cheese, plus a dash of red (cayenne) pepper.

Curried Apple Rice
Sauté 1 finely chopped tart apple in butter with 2 teaspoons curry powder and a dash of lemon juice. Add to cooked rice.

Herbed Rice
Add 1/4 cup chopped fresh parsley alone or with 2 tablespoons of other chopped fresh herbs to cooked rice.

Saffron Rice
Add 1/4 to 1/2 teaspoon powdered saffon to the chicken stock before cooking rice.

Vegetable Rice
Add diced fresh or sun-dried tomatoes; steamed peas, red, green or yellow bell peppers; or mushrooms, which have been sautéed in a little butter to cooked rice.

Tip
Keep cooked rice warm in a covered colander over simmering water.

RISOTTO

This classic Italian technique makes a delicious creamy rice dish that stands on its own. The grains of Arborio rice are a bit thick and short, so it holds up to long cooking without becoming mushy.

4 to 5 cups Chicken Stock (page 23)
1/4 cup unsalted butter
1 tablespoon olive oil
1 small onion, finely chopped
1-1/2 cups rice, preferably Italian Arborio rice
1/2 cup freshly grated Parmesan cheese
1/4 teaspoon salt or to taste
1/8 teaspoon freshly ground white pepper

Bring stock to a steady simmer in a medium-size saucepan. In a separate heavy saucepan, melt butter with oil over medium heat. Add onion; sauté until softened, but not browned. Add rice, stir to coat well and sauté 1 or 2 minutes. Begin adding simmering broth 1/2 cup at a time, stirring all the while, never adding more until the preceding batch has been absorbed and the rice begins to dry out. This procedure will take 30 to 45 minutes to complete. When done, rice will have absorbed as much liquid as possible and will be creamy but *al dente,* firm to the bite. Remove from heat. Stir in cheese and season with salt and pepper. Makes 4 servings.

VARIATIONS

MUSHROOM RISOTTO
Sauté 1/2 pound wild and/or cultivated mushrooms with onions, adding 1 tablespoon more olive oil.

VEGETABLE RISOTTO
Sauté asparagus, green peas, zucchini or other vegetables with the onions, adding 1 tablespoon more olive oil.

ONION & RICE SOUBISE

This rich and glorious puree is a far cry from a "simple starch," but it's sure to turn the most humble fowl into a French-style feast.

2 pounds onions
5 tablespoons unsalted butter
3/4 cup white long-grain rice
2 cups Chicken Stock (page 23)
1 teaspoon salt
1/3 teaspoon freshly ground white pepper
1/3 cup whipping cream

Peel and coarsely slice onions. Melt 3 tablespoons of the butter in a 2-quart saucepan over medium heat, add onions and cook until softened but not browned. Stir in rice. Add stock, salt and pepper. Cover and simmer 30 minutes. Puree mixture in a food processor, adding cream and the remaining 2 tablespoons butter. Return to saucepan and reheat over very low heat. Adjust seasonings to taste. Makes 4 to 6 servings.

BASIC WILD RICE

Wild rice is actually a seed from a wild grass and not rice at all. The difficulty in harvesting this particular seed, as well as its nutty, chewy flavor, justifies its price.

4 cups Chicken Stock (page 23) and/or water
1 cup wild rice
1 teaspoon salt
2 to 3 tablespoons unsalted butter (optional)

In a 2-quart saucepan, bring stock to a boil over medium heat. Rinse rice in a colander under cold running water and add to stock with salt. Reduce heat to medium-low and boil, uncovered, until rice is tender, about 35 minutes. Drain and toss with butter, if desired. Makes about 3-1/2 cups.

DIRTY RICE

A southern classic that is so called because the rice takes on a brownish color when cooked with the livers and gizzards.

3 tablespoons olive oil
8 ounces chicken livers, fat removed, finely chopped
8 ounces chicken gizzards, fat removed, finely chopped
1 large onion, coarsely chopped
1 small green bell pepper, coarsely chopped
4 celery stalks, coarsely chopped
3 large garlic cloves, minced
2 teaspoons salt
1/2 teaspoon freshly ground black pepper
1/8 teaspoon red (cayenne) pepper
2 cups water
1 cup uncooked long-grain rice
1/2 cup chopped green onions
1/2 cup minced parsley

Heat olive oil in a heavy 4- or 5-quart dutch oven over medium heat. Add livers, gizzards, onion, bell pepper, celery, garlic, salt, black pepper and cayenne. Reduce heat to low and cook, stirring occasionally, about 30 minutes. Increase heat to medium and add water; bring to a boil. Stir in rice, cover and reduce heat to low. After 15 minutes, add green onions and parsley and cook, covered, another 5 minutes. Remove from heat and rest 5 minutes before serving. Makes 6 to 8 servings.

BULGUR

Bulgur is cracked wheat, with a nutty, chewy flavor reminiscent of brown rice.

2 tablespoons unsalted butter
1 cup bulgur wheat
Salt and freshly ground pepper to taste
2 cups Chicken Stock (page 23) and/or water

Melt butter in a 1-1/2- to 2-quart saucepan over medium heat. Add bulgur and stir 2 minutes to coat well. Add salt, pepper and stock, cover and simmer 15 minutes or until liquid is absorbed and bulgur is tender. Makes 4 servings.

BRAISED BULGUR

Vary this Middle Eastern delight by adding chopped fresh herbs, such as parsley and sage.

1/2 cup unsalted butter
1 onion, minced
1 cup bulgur wheat
2 cups Chicken Stock (page 23)
1 teaspoon salt
1/4 teaspoon freshly ground pepper

Preheat oven to 350F (175C). Melt butter in a medium-size flameproof casserole dish over medium heat. Add onion; sauté until softened but not brown, then add bulgur and cook, stirring, until golden, 2 or 3 minutes. Add stock, salt and pepper. Bake 30 minutes, covered, until liquid has been absorbed and bulgur is tender. Fluff with a fork before serving. Makes 4 servings.

BOILED COUSCOUS

Couscous, sometimes known as Moroccan pasta, is the Arabic word for finely ground semolina. This should not be confused with the North African lamb stew of the same name. Couscous can be found in many delicatessens, gourmet shops and Middle Eastern groceries.

4 cups Chicken Stock (page 23) and/or water
2 cups couscous
1/2 cup unsalted butter
1 teaspoon salt

In a large heavy saucepan set over medium-high heat, bring stock to a rapid boil and gradually pour in couscous, stirring constantly, to prevent lumping. Cook 2 or 3 minutes, stirring constantly. Mix in butter and salt. Remove from heat, cover and let stand 10 to 15 minutes, or until moisture is absorbed. Fluff with a fork before serving. Makes 6 servings.

POLENTA

This yellow cornmeal mush often takes the place of bread or pasta in Northern Italy. Fresh creamy polenta is the ultimate comfort food, and leftover polenta takes on a whole new identity when baked or grilled. Polenta becomes firm very quickly, so any leftovers should be formed into a shape that can be easily sliced when cold.

4 cups Chicken Stock (page 23), and/or water
1 teaspoon salt
1 cup polenta (coarsely ground yellow cornmeal)
1/4 cup butter, cut into pieces
Parmesan cheese (optional)

In a 2- to 2-1/2-quart saucepan over medium heat, bring stock to a boil. Add salt and very gradually pour in polenta, stirring constantly until thickened. Transfer to top of a double boiler and continue cooking over medium heat, stirring frequently, about 45 minutes or until the mixture forms a crust on the sides of the double boiler. Blend in butter. Serve immediately in a warm serving bowl as is, or with a sprinkling of Parmesan cheese. Makes 6 servings.

VARIATIONS

POLENTA WITH CHEESE
Add freshly grated cheese, such as Parmesan, Pecorino or Fontina; or crumbled gorgonzola to taste, along with butter at the end of cooking.

BAKED POLENTA PARMIGIANA
Prepare polenta as directed and, while still hot, turn into a buttered 8- or 9-inch-square pan. Smooth top with a knife or spatula and allow to cool. Cut into 2-inch squares and arrange in a single layer in a buttered ovenproof dish. Drizzle with 1/3 cup each of melted unsalted butter and freshly grated Parmesan. Bake, uncovered, 30 minutes at 400F (205C).

FRIED OR GRILLED POLENTA
Form fresh polenta into a shape that can be easily sliced when firm. Cover with plastic wrap and refrigerate. Slice and brush both sides of polenta pieces with melted butter and/or olive oil. Sauté or grill until brown and crusty on the outside.

POLENTA WITH SAUCE
Serve either fresh or grilled polenta with sauce, such as the Tomato Sauce or Mushroom Sauces on pages 138 and 139. The Wild Mushroom Ragout on page 148 would be another great combination.

CHEESY GRITS CASSEROLE

A box of grits in the pantry can be a real "life-saver" when composing impromptu meals. In this case, grits puff into a mock soufflé.

3/4 cup instant cooking grits
3/4 cup milk
3/4 cup Chicken Stock (page 23) and/or water
1/2 teaspoon salt
1/2 cup unsalted butter, cut into pieces
6 ounces Cheddar, Swiss or Jack cheese,
    shredded
3 large eggs, lightly beaten

Preheat oven to 350F (175C). Butter a 1-quart soufflé or other ovenproof dish. Place grits, milk, stock and salt in the top of a double boiler set over medium heat and cook, stirring occasionally, until grits have absorbed liquid. Remove from heat and stir in butter and cheese. Cool 5 to 10 minutes, then beat in eggs and turn into buttered 1-quart dish. Bake 30 to 40 minutes, until top is lightly browned. Makes 6 servings.

BASIC PASTA DOUGH

Pasta is a favorite with nearly all nationalities. And once you've experienced the incomparable texture and flavor of homemade egg pasta, you're sure to become a convert. Rather than paying high prices at delicatessens and gourmet shops, learn to make your own at home. Making pasta with family and friends can be a fun project with a delicious ending.

2 cups unbleached all-purpose flour
2 large eggs
1 tablespoon olive oil
1 teaspoon plus 2 tablespoons salt

Mound flour on a clean, dry board and make a well in the center with your fist. In a small bowl, lightly beat together the eggs, oil and 1 teaspoon salt. Pour into the well and use your fingers to incorporate the flour until the mass holds together. Knead until dough is smooth and elastic, about 10 minutes. Place dough in a bowl, cover with plastic wrap and rest at room tempera-ture at least 30 minutes. This will relax the gluten in the flour so the pasta will be easier to roll. If using a hand turned pasta machine, roll according to manufacturer's instructions. Otherwise, flour a clean surface and rolling pin and quickly roll the dough until 1/8 to 1/16 inch thick. To facilitate rolling, you may want to first divide the dough into 2 or more batches. Be sure to cover the dough you are not working with so it doesn't dry out. Roll up the flattened dough as you would a jellyroll and cut into desired widths with a swift cut from a clean, sharp knife. Let cut pasta dry, uncovered, on a flour-dusted towel 15 minutes before cooking. To cook, bring 6 to 8 quarts of water to a rolling boil, add 2 tablespoons salt and pasta; cook 1 to 2 minutes, depending upon the thickness and shape of the pasta. Drain and serve. Makes 1 pound.

VARIATIONS

SPINACH PASTA
Cook, drain and mince 1/2 pound fresh spinach or use half of 1 (10-oz.) package of frozen spinach, thawed and well drained. Add to egg mixture. If dough is too sticky, work in a bit more flour.

HERB PASTA
Add 2 tablespoons finely minced fresh herbs of choice (or 2 teaspoons dried leaf herbs) to egg mixture.

SAFFRON PASTA
Grind 2 pinches of saffron in a mortar and pestle and add 2 teaspoons lemon juice or hot water to blend. Let stand about 15 minutes. Add saffron mixture to egg mixture. If dough is too sticky, work in a bit more flour.

TOMATO PASTA
Add 2 tablespoons of tomato paste to egg mixture. If the dough is too sticky, work in a bit more flour.

SZECHUAN PEPPER PASTA

In a wok or skillet over medium heat, toast 2 tablespoons of Szechuan peppercorns until fragrant, 1 to 2 minutes. Crush in a peppermill or mortar and pestle before adding to egg mixture.

RED CHILI PEPPER PASTA

Add 2 teaspoons finely crushed red pepper flakes to egg mixture.

CARROT OR BEET PASTA

Steam or boil 1 carrot or 1 beet until very soft, then puree. Add 2 tablespoons vegetable puree to egg mixture. If dough is too sticky, work in a bit more flour.

BELL PEPPER PASTA

Roast peppers of any color to peel them, then puree. Add 2 tablespoons bell pepper puree to egg mixture. If dough is too sticky, work in a bit more flour.

SPICED PASTA

Add 2 teaspoons of dried ground spices (such as ginger, curry, paprika or chili powder) to egg mixture.

METRIC CHART

Comparison to Metric Measure

When You Know	Symbol	Multiply By	To Find	Symbol
teaspoons	tsp	5.0	milliliters	ml
tablespoons	tbsp	15.0	milliliters	ml
fluid ounces	fl. oz.	30.0	milliliters	ml
cups	c	0.24	liters	l
pints	pt.	0.47	liters	l
quarts	qt.	0.95	liters	l
ounces	oz.	28.0	grams	g
pounds	lb.	0.45	kilograms	kg
Fahrenheit	F	5/9 (after subtracting 32)	Celsius	C

Fahrenheit to Celsius

F	C
200—205	95
220—225	105
245—250	120
275	135
300—305	150
325—330	165
345—350	175
370—375	190
400—405	205
425—430	220
445—450	230
470—475	245
500	260

Liquid Measure to Milliliters

1/4 teaspoon	=	1.25 milliliters
1/2 teaspoon	=	2.5 milliliters
3/4 teaspoon	=	3.75 milliliters
1 teaspoon	=	5.0 milliliters
1-1/4 teaspoons	=	6.25 milliliters
1-1/2 teaspoons	=	7.5 milliliters
1-3/4 teaspoons	=	8.75 milliliters
2 teaspoons	=	10.0 milliliters
1 tablespoon	=	15.0 milliliters
2 tablespoons	=	30.0 milliliters

Liquid Measure to Liters

1/4 cup	=	0.06 liters
1/2 cup	=	0.12 liters
3/4 cup	=	0.18 liters
1 cup	=	0.24 liters
1-1/4 cups	=	0.3 liters
1-1/2 cups	=	0.36 liters
2 cups	=	0.48 liters
2-1/2 cups	=	0.6 liters
3 cups	=	0.72 liters
3-1/2 cups	=	0.84 liters
4 cups	=	0.96 liters
4-1/2 cups	=	1.08 liters
5 cups	=	1.2 liters
5-1/2 cups	=	1.32 liters

INDEX